ISBN 978-0-243-44154-9
PIBN 10798848

1 MONTH OF
FREE
READING

at

www.ForgottenBooks.com

By purchasing this book you are eligible for one month membership to ForgottenBooks.com, giving you unlimited access to our entire collection of over 1,000,000 titles via our web site and mobile apps.

To claim your free month visit:

www.forgottenbooks.com/free798848

English
Français
Deutsche
Italiano
Español
Português

www.forgottenbooks.com

Mythology Photography **Fiction**
Fishing Christianity **Art** Cooking
Essays Buddhism Freemasonry
Medicine **Biology** Music **Ancient**
Egypt Evolution Carpentry Physics
Dance Geology **Mathematics** Fitness
Shakespeare **Folklore** Yoga Marketing
Confidence Immortality Biographies
Poetry **Psychology** Witchcraft
Electronics Chemistry History **Law**
Accounting **Philosophy** Anthropology
Alchemy Drama Quantum Mechanics
Atheism Sexual Health **Ancient History**
Entrepreneurship Languages Sport
Paleontology Needlework Islam
Metaphysics Investment Archaeology
Parenting Statistics Criminology
Motivational

The American Legion Weekly

NOVEMBER 28, 1919
Vol. 1   No. 22

Five Cents a Copy
Two Dollars a Year

If you had been on the Arizona

HERE she comes, homeward bound, with "a bone in her teeth," and a record for looking into many strange ports in six short months.

If you had been one of her proud sailors you would have left New York City in *January*, been at Guantanamo, Cuba, in *February*, gone ashore at Port of Spain, Trinidad, in *March* and stopped at Brest, France, in *April* to bring the President home. In *May* the Arizona swung at her anchor in the harbor of Smyrna, Turkey. In *June* she rested under the shadow of Gibraltar and in *July* she was back in New York harbor.

Her crew boasts that no millionaire tourist ever globe-trotted like this. There was one period of four weeks in which the crew saw the coasts of North America, South America, Europe, Asia and Africa.

An enlistment in the navy

gives you a chance at the education of travel. Your mind is quickened by contact with new people, new places, new ways of doing things.

Pay begins the day you join. On board ship a man is always learning. There is work to be done and he is taught to do it well. Trade schools develop skill, industry and business ability. Work and play are planned by experts. Thirty days furlough each year with full pay. The food is fine. A full outfit of clothing is provided free. Promotion is unlimited for men of brains. You can enlist for two years and come out broader, stronger, abler. "The Navy made a man of me" is an expression often heard.

Apply at any recruiting station if you are over 17. There you will get full information. If you can't find the recruiting station, ask your Postmaster. He knows.

Shove off!
Join the U. S. Navy

How I Improved My Memory In One Evening

The Amazing Experience of Victor Jones

"Of course I place you! Mr. Addison Sims of Seattle.

"If I remember correctly—and I *do* remember correctly—Mr. Burroughs, the lumberman, introduced me to you at the luncheon of the Seattle Rotary Club three years ago in May. This is a pleasure indeed! I haven't laid eyes on you since that day. How is the grain business? And how did that amalgamation work out?"

The assurance of this speaker—in the crowded corridor of the Hotel McAlpin—compelled me to turn and look at him, though I must say it is not my usual habit to "listen in" even in a hotel lobby.

"He is David M. Roth, the most famous memory expert in the United States," said my friend Kennedy, answering my question before I could get it out. "He will show you a lot more wonderful things than that, before the evening is over."

And he did.

As we went into the banquet room the toastmaster was introducing a long line of the guests to Mr. Roth. I got in line and when it came my turn, Mr. Roth asked, "What are your initials, Mr. Jones, and your business connection and telephone number?" Why he asked this, I learned later, when he picked out from the crowd the 60 men he had met two hours before and called each by name without a mistake. What is more, he named each man's business and telephone number, for good measure.

I won't tell you all the other amazing things this man did except to tell how he called back, without a minute's hesitation, long lists of numbers, bank clearings, prices, lot numbers, parcel post rates and anything else the guests gave him in rapid order.

****

When I met Mr. Roth—which you may be sure I did the first chance I got—he rather bowled me over by saying, in his quiet, modest way:

"There is nothing miraculous about my remembering anything I want to remember whether it be names, faces, figures, facts, or something I have read in a magazine.

"*You can do this just as easily as I do.* Anyone with an average mind can learn quickly to do exactly the same things which seem so miraculous when I do them.

"My own memory," continued Mr. Roth, "was originally very faulty. Yes, it was—a really *poor* memory. On meeting a man I would lose his name in thirty seconds, while now there are probably 10,000 men and women in the United States, whose names I can call instantly on meeting them."

"That is all right for you, Mr. Roth," I interrupted, "you have given years to it. But how about me?"

"Mr. Jones," he replied, "I can teach you the secret of a good memory in one evening. This is not a guess, because I have done it with thousands of pupils. In the first of

seven simple lessons which I have prepared for home study, I show you the basic principle of my whole system and you will find it—not hard work as you might fear—but just like playing a fascinating game. I will prove it to you."

He didn't have to prove it. His Course did; I got it the very next day from his publishers, the Independent Corporation.

When I tackled the first lesson, I suppose I was the most surprised man in forty-eight states to find that I had learned in about one hour how to remember a list of one hundred words so that I could call them off forward and back without a single mistake.

The first lesson *stuck.* And so did the other six.

Read this letter from Terence J. McManus, of the firm of Olcott, Bonynge, McManus & Ernst, Attorneys and Counsellors at Law, 170 Broadway, and one of the most famous trial lawyers in New York:

"May I take occasion to state that I regard your service in giving this system to the world as a public benefaction. The wonderful simplicity of the method and the ease with which its principles may be acquired, especially appeal to me. I may add that I already had occasion to test the effectiveness of the first two lessons in the preparation for trial of an important action in which I am about to engage."

Mr. McManus didn't put it a bit too strong. The Roth Course is priceless! I can absolutely *count* on my memory now. I can call the name of most any man I have met before—and I am getting better all the time. I can remember any figures I wish to remember. Telephone numbers come to mind instantly, once I have filed them by Mr. Roth's easy method. Street addresses are just as easy.

The old fear of forgetting (you know what that is) has vanished. I used to be "scared stiff" on my feet—because I wasn't *sure.* I couldn't remember what I wanted to say.

Now I am sure of myself, and confident, and "easy as an old shoe" when I get on my feet at the club, or at a banquet, or in a business meeting, or in any social gathering.

Perhaps the most enjoyable part of it all is that I have become a good conversationalist—and I used to be as silent as a sphinx when I got into a crowd of people who knew things.

Now I can call up like a flash of lightning most any fact I want right at the instant I need it most. I used to think a "hair trigger" memory belonged only to the prodigy and genius. Now I see that every man of us has that kind of a memory if he only knows how to make it work right.

I tell you it is a wonderful thing, after groping around in the dark for so many years to be able to switch the big searchlight on your mind and *see* instantly everything you want to remember.

This Roth course will do wonders in your office.

Since we took it up you never hear anyone in *our* office say "I guess" or "I think it was about so much" or "I forget that right now" or "I can't remember" or "I must look up his name." Now they are right there with the answer—like a shot.

Have you ever heard of "Multigraph" Smith? Real name H. Q. Smith, Division Manager of the Multigraph Sales Company, Ltd., in Montreal. Here is just a bit from a letter of his that I saw last week:

"Here is the whole thing in a nutshell: Mr. Roth has a most remarkable Memory Course. It is simple, and easy as falling off a log. Yet with one hour a day of practice, anyone—I don't care who he is—can improve his Memory 100% in a week and 1,000% in six months."

My advice to you is don't wait another minute. Send to Independent Corporation for Mr. Roth's amazing course and see what a wonderful memory you have got. Your dividends in *increased earning power* will be enormous.

VICTOR JONES.

SEND NO MONEY

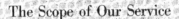

AMERICAN LEGION DIRECTORY
National and Local Representatives of the Legion

Joint National Executive Committee of Thirty-Four

HENRY D. LINDSLEY, TEX., *Chairman*   ERIC FISHER WOOD, PA., *Secretary*
BENNETT C. CLARK, MO., *Vice-Chairman*   GASPAR G. BACON, MASS., *Treasurer*
JOHN W. PRENTISS, *Chairman National Finance Committee*

WILLIAM S. BEAM, N. C.
CHARLES H. BRENT, N. Y.
WILLIAM H. BROWN, CONN.
G. EDWARD BUXTON, JR., R. I.
PHILO. C. CALHOUN, CONN.
RICHARD DERBY, N. Y.
FRANKLIN D'OLIER, PA.
L. H. EVRIDGE, TEX.
MILTON FOREMAN, ILL.
RUBY D. GARRETT, MO.
FRED A. GRIFFITH, OKLA.
ROY C. HAINES, ME.

EDWARD A. HEFFERNAN, N. Y.
J. F. J. HERBERT, MASS.
ROY HOFFMAN, OKLA.
FRED B. HUMPHREYS, N. MEX.
JOHN W. INZER, ALA.
STUART S. JANNEY, MD.
LUKE LEA, TENN.
HENRY LEONARD, COL.
THOMAS W. MILLER, DEL.
OGDEN MILLS, JR., N. Y.
EDWARD MYERS, PA.
RICHARD PATTERSON, JR., N. Y.

WILLIAM G. PRICE, JR., PA.
S. A. RITCHIE, N. Y.
THEODORE ROOSEVELT, JR., N. Y.
DALE SHAW, IOWA
ALBERT A. SPRAGUE, ILL.
DANIEL G. STIVERS, MONT.
JOHN J. SULLIVAN, WASH.
H. J. TURNEY, OHIO.
GEORGE A. WHITE, ORE.
GEORGE H. WOOD, OHIO.

National Headquarters of The American Legion and the Editorial Department of The American Legion Weekly are at 19 West 44th St., New York City, N. Y.

RETURNING SOLDIERS

Get in touch with your local post. If there is no local post, write to your state chairman. Join The American Legion.

You helped give the Hun all that was coming to him. Have you got everything that is coming to you? Have you had any trouble with your *War Risk Allotment or Allowance, Quartermaster or Navy Allotment, Compensation, Insurance, Liberty Bonds, Bonus, Travel Pay, Back Pay?*

The American Legion is ready to help straighten out your accounts. Write or tell your troubles to your State War Risk Officer of The American Legion. Write in care of your State Secretary.

STATE OFFICERS

ALABAMA—*Chairman*, Matt W. Murphy, 1st Nat. Bank Bldg., Birmingham; *Secretary*, Herman W. Thompson, care of Adjutant-General, Montgomery.

ARIZONA—*Chairman*, Andrew P. Martin, Tucson; *Secretary*, Dudley W. Windes, Phoenix.

ARKANSAS—*Chairman*, J. J. Harrison, 207 W. 3rd St., Little Rock; *Secretary*, Granville Burrow, Little Rock.

CALIFORNIA—*President*, David P. Barrows, 926 Flood Bldg., San Francisco; *Secretary*, Fred F. Bebergall, 926 Flood Bldg., San Francisco.

COLORADO—*Chairman*, H. A. Saidy, Colorado Springs; *Secretary*, Morton M. David, 401 Empire Bldg., Denver.

CONNECTICUT—*Chairman*, P. C. Calhoun, 888 Main St., Bridgeport; *Secretary*, Thomas J. Bannigan, Asylum St., Hartford.

DELAWARE—*Chairman*, Dr. Meredith I. Samuel, 822 West St., Wilmington; *Secretary*, Clarence M. Dillon, Wilmington.

DISTRICT OF COLUMBIA—*Chairman*, E. Lester Jones, 833 Southern Bldg., Washington; *Secretary*, Howard Fisk, 833 Southern Bldg., Washington.

FLORIDA—*Chairman*, A. H. Blanding, Bartow; *Secretary*, S. L. Lowry, Jr., Citizens' Bank Bldg., Tampa.

GEORGIA—*Chairman*, Basil Stockbridge, 405 Postoffice Bldg., Atlanta; *Secretary*, Kirk Smith, 1206 Third National Bank Bldg., Atlanta.

HAWAII—*Commander*, Leonard Withington, care of Advertiser Publishing Co., Honolulu; *Adjutant*, Henry P. O'Sullivan, Public Utilities Commission, Honolulu.

IDAHO—*Chairman*, E. C. Boom, Moscow; *Secretary*, Laverne Collier, Pocatello.

ILLINOIS—*Chairman*, George G. Seaman, Taylorville; *Secretary*, Earl B. Searcy, 205-206 Marquette Bldg., Chicago, Ill.

INDIANA—*Chairman*, Raymond S. Springer, Connersville; *Secretary*, L. Russell Newgent, 518 Hume Mansur Bldg., Indianapolis.

IOWA—*Adjutant*, John MacVicar, 336 Hubbell Bldg., Des Moines.

KANSAS—*Chairman*, Dr. W. A. Phares, 1109 Bitting Bldg., Wichita; *Secretary*, Frank E. Samuel, 135 N. Market St., Wichita.

KENTUCKY—*Chairman*, Henry De Haven Moorman, Hardinsburgh; *Secretary*, D. A. Sachs, 534 West Jefferson St., Louisville.

LOUISIANA—*Chairman*, T. Semmes Walmsley, 721 Hibernia Bank of Louisiana, New Orleans; *Secretary*, Geo. H. H. Pratt, 804 Gravier St., New Orleans.

MAINE—*Chairman*, Albert Greenlaw, Public Utilities Commission, Augusta; *Secretary*, James L. Boyle, 108 Maine St., Waterville.

MARYLAND—*Chairman*, James A. Gary, Jr., 4 Hoen Bldg., Baltimore; *Secretary*, Will Wayne, 4 Hoen Bldg., Baltimore.

MASSACHUSETTS—*Commander*, Edward L. Logan, South Boston, Mass.; *Secretary*, Leo A. Spillane, 84 State St., Boston.

MICHIGAN—*Chairman*, George C. Waldo, 401-5 Equity Bldg., Detroit; *Secretary*, Lyle D. Tabor, 401-5 Equity Bldg., Detroit.

MINNESOTA—*Chairman*, Harrison Fuller, care of St. Paul Dispatch, St. Paul; *Secretary*, Horace G. Whitmore, 603 Guardian Life Bldg., St. Paul.

MISSISSIPPI—*Chairman*, Alexander Fitzhugh, Vicksburg; *Secretary*, Edward S. Butts, Vicksburg.

MISSOURI—*Commander*, Sidney Houston, Kansas City; *Adjutant*, Edward J. Cahill, Public Service Commission, Jefferson City.

MONTANA—*Chairman*, Charles E. Pew, care of Wight & Pew, Helena; *Secretary*, Ben W. Barnett, 1014 Bedford St., Helena.

NEBRASKA—*President*, Earl M. Cline, Nebraska City.

NEVADA—*Chairman*, J. G. Scrugham, State Capitol, Carson City; *Secretary*, H. M. Payne, Carson City, Nev.

NEW HAMPSHIRE—*Chairman*, Orville Cain, Keene; *Secretary*, Frank J. Abbott, 6 Pickering Bldg., Manchester.

NEW JERSEY—*Chairman*, Robert Brown, 776 Broad St., Newark; *Secretary*, Thomas Goldingay, 776 Broad St., Newark.

NEW MEXICO—*Chairman*, Charles M. De Bremon, Roswell; *Secretary*, Harry Howard Dorman, Santa Fe.

NEW YORK—*Chairman*, Russell E. Sard, 140 Nassau St., New York City; *Secretary*, Wade H. Hayes, 140 Nassau St., New York.

NORTH CAROLINA—*Chairman*, C. K. Burgess, 607 Commercial Bank Bldg., Raleigh; *Secretary*, C. A. Gosney, Raleigh.

NORTH DAKOTA—*Commander*, M. Dawson, Beach; *Secretary*, Jack Williams, Grand Forks.

OHIO—*Chairman*, F. C. Galbraith, Adj. Gen. Office, State House, Columbus; *Secretary*, Chalmers R. Wilson, Adj. Gen. Office, State House, Columbus.

OKLAHOMA—*Commander*, H. H. Hagen, Texas Co., Tulsa; *Adjutant*, Eugene Adkins, 711 Barnes Bldg., Muskogee.

OREGON—*Chairman*, Wm. B. Follett, Eugene; *Secretary*, Ed. J. Eivers, 444½ Larabee St., Portland.

PENNSYLVANIA—*Chairman*, George F. Tyler, 121 S. 5th St., Philadelphia; *Secretary*, Wm. G. Murdock, 121 S. 5th St., Philadelphia.

PHILIPPINE ISLANDS—*Chairman*, Robert R. Landon, Manila; *Secretary*, Amos D. Haskell, Manila.

RHODE ISLAND—*Chairman*, Alexander H. Johnson, City Hall, Providence; *Secretary*, Rush Sturges, Central Fire Station, Exchange Place, Providence.

SOUTH CAROLINA—*Chairman*, Julius H. Walker, Columbia; *Secretary*, Irvine F. Belser, Columbia.

SOUTH DAKOTA—*Chairman*, M. L. Shade, Mitchell; *Secretary*, C. J. Harris, 212 Boyce Greeley Bldg., Sioux Falls.

TENNESSEE—*Chairman*, Roan Waring, Bank of Commerce & Trust Co. Bldg., Memphis; *Secretary*, Wm. J. Bacon, 35 Goodbar Bldg., Memphis.

TEXAS—*Commander*, Henry Hutchings, 111½ E. 10th Street, Ft. Worth; *Secretary*, Chas. W. Scruggs, 722 Gunter Bldg., San Antonio.

UTAH—*Chairman*, Wesley E. King, Judge Bldg., Salt Lake City; *Secretary*, Baldwin Robertson, 604 Newhouse Bldg., Salt Lake City.

VERMONT—*Chairman*, H. Nelson Jackson, Burlington; *Secretary*, Joseph H. Fountain, 139 Church Street, Burlington.

VIRGINIA—*Chairman*, Wm. A. Stuart, Big Stone Gap; *Secretary*, C. Brocke Pollard, 1114 Mutual Bldg., Richmond.

WASHINGTON—*Chairman*, vacant until state convention; *Secretary*, George R. Drever, care of Adj. Gen. Office, Armory, Seattle.

WEST VIRGINIA—*Chairman*, Jackson Arnold, Department of Public S fety, Box 405, Charleston; *Secretary*, Charles McCamic, 904 National Bank of W. Va. Bldg., Wheeling.

WISCONSIN—*Chairman*, John C. Davis, 210 Plankenton Avenue, Milwaukee; *Secretary*, R. M. Gibson, 8 MacKinnon Block, Grand Rapids.

WYOMING—*Chairman*, Chas. S. Hill, Cheyenne; *Secretary*, Harry Fisher, Casper.

THE AMERICAN LEGION WEEKLY is published weekly by THE LEGION PUBLISHING CORPORATION, 511 Eleventh Street, N. W., Washington, D. C. Entered as second-class matter November 3, 1919, at the Post Office at Washington, D. C., under the Act of March 3, 1879.

The American Legion Weekly

Official Publication of
The American Legion

OWNED EXCLUSIVELY BY THE AMERICAN LEGION

The Voice of the New Day

Having Spoken for Great Things, the Legion Must Now Bend to Its Great Task and Achieve Them

By MARQUIS JAMES

THE life of a nation is the sum total of its experiences. The American nation has been subject to a kaleidoscopic series of new experiences within the past three years. What was to be the effect on the national life? The question has issued from many lips and many pens during the year past.

Political seers gazed into the crystal of recent events, hoping to read mirrored there the answer, but they gazed in vain. What they saw was a victorious fighting force of 4,800,000 men in the process of rapid dissolution. From the camps, from the fleet, from the battle-grounds in foreign lands, they were breaking away in large numbers and scattering individually to their homes. By this process vanished the mighty forces of land and sea, and in the fulness of time the men and women who had comprised those forces were back at the scenes of their old occupations.

The cycle was thus completed in a little more than two years, and a new one begun. The new cycle proved a poser to the prophet of national futures. The man who came back from the fighting services was a different tempered person than he was when he went away. He was the product of his share of the new experiences which had been going around. They had altered and reshaped him, so that he found it difficult to fit back into the old niche to which he had conformed so snugly before he had gone out from home and bid for his cut of the hazards of war.

Then came the question: What will be the effect of these new experiences on the future of the American nation?

The tenor of the answer was doubtful. The country quivered with the restlessness of four million individuals who found themselves strangers to their own homes. On the part of the four million just returned from service it was a perfectly natural restlessness that was the direct consequence of their experiences. But to another class the situation afforded an opportunity which spelled peril to the country. Those professional breeders of tainted restlessness, which is the product only of their evil and abortive minds— those natural enemies of government and orderly institutions seized upon the situation to begin a sinister campaign. Bolshevism, the word, christened in the blood of a wayward and hopeless Russia, came and took its place in the speaking vocabulary of Americans. Bolshevism, the fact, skulked in the shadows of the sacred symbols for whose perpetuation we have so recently fought.

WITH things come to this pass the gazers noted in the crystal a new phenomenon. The returned veterans of the great war were banding themselves together. The nucleus about which they gathered had come from overseas, where it was created by a few men about to start home. Slowly at first, but steadily and surely the new body gained in size, as a snowball does when it rolls downhill. It became successively a project, an incident, a possibility, and finally a factor in American life.

A factor for what? It was just another way of putting the old inquiry as to the effects our war experiences would have on the life of the nation.

As before, the question was without an answer, save for those given at the risk of the giver. No one could speak for The American Legion, because The American Legion had not found its voice. Individuals of the Legion might speak, and they did, and their speech was reassuring, but the Legion was mute. The Paris caucus was conceived in the name of

7

high ideals, but whether those ideals were representative of the ideals which had sprung from the new experiences of our citizen soldiery there was no means of divining, because that caucus was not sufficiently inclusive. The St. Louis caucus was fairly representative of an element of former service men who saw the immediate need of a great organization of their comrades, but the great mass of ex-service men had not yet been touched.

But from the time of the St. Louis meeting the Legion grew apace. The spirit of the mass was caught, and from a membership of a million the Legion, now a powerful factor, selected spokesmen to go to Minneapolis and speak the voice and announce the will of their constituents.

The silence has been broken. The Legion has spoken, and it has not mumbled its words. In tones vibrant with the fervor of irrepressible Americanism it has declared its position and taken its stand. It has laid down a platform which is without parallel among the works of American assemblages and has thrown a million strong men and women into the line in support of its declaration. At one step The American Legion, by the deliberations of its representatives at Minneapolis, has placed itself at the head of the fight for those things which now are the dearest concerns of every true citizen of this republic.

IN THE records of the Minneapolis convention the world has the insight into the effect America's new experiences are destined to have on the country's future. There can be no doubt about that. It is discernible with the convention only a week in perspective. That convention was the will of a million men and women who felt those new experiences the keenest of all. Never in the history of the world has there been anything like the first constitutional convention of The American Legion, where a million men, fresh from a war, pooled their sentiments, announced them, and stood joined to fight for the realization of what their experiences tell them is right.

In a dispatch from Minneapolis last week the writer endeavored to epitomize the principal achievements of the convention. Time and space would admit no more than the briefest outline of the great work that was done. Any one of a dozen recommendations which proceeded from the convention is a study in itself in the making of a better America.

Take as an illustration the convention's recommendation for the establishment of the National Americanism Commission of The American Legion. The project has almost unlimited possibilities. It can make the force of the Legion felt in every community that lives under the Stars and Stripes. That members of the Legion may grasp the scope and aims of this enterprise the recommendation is given in full in the language of the resolution which the convention, by unanimous vote, adopted:

WE RECOMMEND the establishment of a National Americanism Commission of The American Legion whose duty shall be the endeavor to realize in the United States the basic ideal of this Legion of one hundred per cent Americanism, through the planning, establishment and conduct of a continuous, constructive, educational system designed to (1) Combat all anti-American tendencies, activities and propaganda; (2) work for the education of immigrants, prospective American citizens and alien residents, in the principles of Americanism; (3) inculcate the ideals of Americanism in the citizen population, particularly the basic American principle that the interests of all the people are above those of any special interest or any so-called class or section of the people; (4) spread throughout the people of the nation information as to the real nature and principles of American government; (5) foster the teaching of Americanism in all schools.

"For the purpose stated the commission shall submit to the National Executive Committee a plan, and from time to time supplementary plans, which may include a national advertising campaign, the publication of literature, the organization of lecture courses, cooperation with schools and other agencies, and such other means of carrying out the purpose outlined as may be appropriate.

"Upon approval by the National Executive Committee the commission shall proceed upon the approved activities.

"But no funds shall be used for this purpose except those specifically appropriated by the Legion or its properly constituted authorities for the appropriation of funds, or which shall be raised with the approval of the National Executive Committee from members of the Legion only.

"The commission may recommend a system of cooperating committees or officers in state branches or posts.

"The commission shall be elected by the National Executive Committee immediately after this convention and shall consist of not more than fifteen members who shall hold office for one year, or until the next National Executive Committee to employ such officers or staff as shall be approved by that committee.

"The committee further recommends:

"That, as the preliminary organization and planning of the commission will take time, meanwhile the local posts of The American Legion be urged to organize immediately for the purpose of meeting the insidious propaganda of Bolshevism, I. W. W.-ism, radicalism and all other anti-Americanisms, by taking up the problems of:

"1. Detecting anti-American activities everywhere and seizing every opportunity, everywhere to speak plainly and openly for one hundred per cent Americanism and for nothing less.

"2. Making direct appeals to legal authority to take such lawful steps as may be necessary to correct local conditions everywhere.

"3. Making every member of each local post a constructive force in the upbuilding of a vital knowledge of the principles of the Constitution of the United States and of the processes of law and order obtaining under that Constitution.

"4. Showing to every person contaminated by un-American prejudice that the welfare of all the people is really the best interest of any class, and that government must be conceived in terms of all the people and not for the benefit of relatively small classes."

THAT document is the echo of the new experiences of a million men. In spirit it is typical of the Minneapolis convention, which did nothing more or less than interpret those experiences. National Commander D'Olier deemed the passage of that resolution one of the most significant acts of the convention, and brought the matter of the creation of the National Americanism Commission of (Continued on page 30)

POLICIES *not* POLITICS

America's Army Must Fight On

The Legion's Battle Has Just Begun

By FRANKLIN D'OLIER
National Commander, The American Legion

THE American Legion has gone over the top and reached its first objective. This is not a time, however, for words. It is not going to halt and dig in, and survey with complacency what thus far has been accomplished. The future is too pregnant with great tasks which claim our energies, for though the Legion emerged from the first constitutional convention at Minneapolis a recognized power in the land, it must fulfil the obligations it contracted and measure up to the fine ideals to which it subscribed.

My comrades of The American Legion, I greet you. It is not only a great honor, but a distinguished privilege which your representatives have conferred upon me, and I can only repeat to you what I have already tried to express to them—my heartfelt appreciation.

The convention which recently completed its labors always will be regarded as one of the most momentous in the history of the United States and of the American race. In its interpretation in concrete acts of the high purposes for which our organization was founded, it has presented to the Legion and to every member a work of service, not only to our comrades but to the nation itself for which so recently we were willing to give our lives.

The war witnessed a triumph of ideals and policies which must ever remain triumphant. Battles are not always won on fields of fire, nor nations strengthened or weakened as the consequence of victories or reverses at arms. The fight we fought in France and elsewhere during the great war must be kept up— and that is what the Legion proposes to do. It is not hard for some to go to war when the vision of the world is centered upon the warrior in uniform. It is harder to fight the quiet and less spectacular fight for those same ideals at home and in the ordinary walks of life. Yet that is what the Legion proposes to do, and what it will do.

Our work is only begun. We have just scratched the surface. The constructive measures to be accomplished in the coming year are enormous, but it is an inspiration to know that the spirit of clear thinking, fair play, cooperation and sound judgment—the "buddy spirit"—which prevailed at the convention, merely was a manifestation of the spirit that pervades the Legion and every member of every local post of our great organization. It is that spirit which assures our success and leaves not the slightest doubt in my mind that we

The American Legion elected, as its first national commander, one of the men who conceived its formation in Paris. Franklin D'Olier was born in Burlington, N. J., April 28, 1877. He is the head of a cotton and cotton yarn commission firm in Philadelphia. He was commissioned in the Quartermaster Corps as a captain in April, 1917, and went to France in August where he was detailed on salvage work. He was promoted to major, then lieutenant-colonel and assigned to the General Staff. He was discharged in April, wearing a D. S. M. Immediately he entered into the organization work of the Legion and since the St. Louis caucus has been in charge of the State Organization Division at National Headquarters.

shall be able to accomplish for our country results as remarkable in peace as they were in war.

The Legion numbers a million men and women who served their country in war. The pronouncements of the convention, which will stand as the most outspoken concourse in the history of this country, were their sentiments. It is a reassuring thought in such times as these. I predict that within a year

that number will be doubled, and with my co-workers I shall work to give realization to that prediction. The word had been coming to headquarters all along for the last few weeks preceding the convention that thousands of ex-service men and women were delaying their decision to join the Legion until they had taken the measure of the organization as it revealed itself at the national convention.

No finer, bolder revelation of patriotism and disinterested Americanism ever has been made in time of peace than that which is to be found in the deliberations and recommendations of the elected representatives of the Legion who met in Minneapolis. It should attract to the ranks of the Legion every one of the 4,800,000 who served, and who served in spirit as well as fact. This little thought I now commend to my comrades throughout the land.

I subscribe without reservation to every word and act of the Minneapolis convention, and I urge upon you to give your deep and thoughtful consideration to the works of that great meeting. I fear no question of doubt in the heart of any Legionnaire regarding the wisdom and patriotism of the actions of that convention, yet every man and woman of The American Legion should inform himself as to what the convention has done, so that he may better appreciate the responsibility and honor that has come to his Legion.

It shall be my sole aim, while I occupy the post of trust and responsibility with which you have honored me, to give action to your wishes as expressed in memorials and resolutions by your representatives at the convention. The Americanism Commission of The American Legion, the creation of which was recommended, to spread and perpetuate the doctrines of one hundred per cent loyalty to flag, government and country, shortly will be brought into being, and adequate provision made for it to carry out the purposes for which it was conceived. Every state and town, every hamlet and farm in the country, shall feel the force of the Legion through this organization.

The Legislative Committee of the Legion at Washington will be instructed to press the desires of the Legion upon Congress and to obtain the enactment of laws which will realize the demands expressed by the convention. These recommendations fall into three general classes: First, those looking toward a better Americanization of the fabric of our (Continued on page 28)

The Great "Paper Bullet" Drive

Laughing the "Prop" out of Propaganda

By RUTHERFORD B. CORBIN

MR. DOOLEY once said German diplomacy was about as subtle as a brickyard. Mr. Dooley was the eminent authority on the use of Irish artillery, but in this case he didn't quite finish the description. German diplomacy generally started like a G. I. can and finished like a dud. Something, perhaps the detonator, failed to go off. It didn't work. It was, as Ben Atwell used to say about plays: there are no bad plays, but sometimes the audience is poorly selected. Once they played "Uncle Tom's Cabin" with a thoroughly good cast, three well-groomed bloodhounds and a real colored man as Uncle Tom, but they played it in Charleston, South Carolina.

Nobody threw anything. They just plain laughed. It was annoying but funny. Nothing to get mad about. But the play wasn't a complete hit. As Kid Gleason of the White Sox said, after the defeat of October 5— "You gotta guess them right."

And from Fritz Von Papen's efforts here in the States straight through to the last number of the *Aerial Messenger* dropped over the Verdun field last fall, Jerry continually guessed wrong, though, like Kid Gleason's team, he kept up trying long after it was but a review of what might have been. The trouble was he forgot we had a sense of humor. Some of his work was coarse, but a lot of it was just funny to the man with a sense of humor.

Once somebody laughed Spain's chivalry away. German propaganda in France laughed itself away. The bird just off K. P. and wanting something to cheer him up scanned the sheets that came down from the skies and said:

"You're trying to kid me."

The editor of the *Aerial Messenger* was a serious minded hombre. He and the Kaiser and the Kaiser's friends who got so used to elevating their hands that the semaphore "U" is now the habitual greeting in East Westphalia, took themselves so seriously that not a one of them got a single laugh out of the whole blooming war.

Staff officers and M. P.s, generals in baby bath-tubs tacked on to their motorcycles; general orders, first sergeants, goldfish, corned willie, duds, those that weren't duds, second position jams, orders to shave every morning, the full pack, the twelve copies of the sailing orders at Brest—you got some pain but a lot of laughs out of some things. And some of them weren't so funny at that.

Which is where the *Aerial Messenger* was *fini*. Mr. G. Propaganda forgot to run a joke column on his sheet. The result was you misunderstood the purpose of his efforts and took the whole thing as a joke.

From the beginning of the war the distribution of the special information to the enemy by airplane was a recognized method of weakened morale. The first aerial propaganda was a British sheet dropped into what once was Lille, setting forth the causes of the war as evinced by the first British White Book. As a diplomatic document it was a gem, but no serious-minded Boche was much interested in who started the war. They already knew and were waking up nights to guess who would finish it. But the British aerial propaganda was good and Jerry was never a slow imitator.

A flock of German planes immediately and forthwith proceeded to float little balloons out of the range of the archies, down on Vimy and Thiepval with their answer, which was the reply of Germany, printed in neat little pamphlets to the effect that Germany was O. K. and didn't start the war at all, but hating war and having no army, somebody crowded them across the line into Belgium.

It was all very good but not as good as it might have been. Every Australian who could read German got a laugh out of it, for every word was printed in German! It took the Boche just three years to find out that his efforts were not being appreciated as they should be and change the text of his remarks from German to English.

The Australian used to spend days trying to get their little aerial messages translated. When he succeeded he usu-

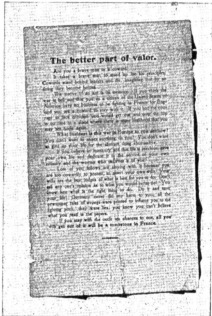

The editor of the Aerial Messenger was a serious minded hombre.

LOTS of the war came fast, but most of it came mighty slow. A good deal was dismal, but you were fairly cheerful, just the same. You usually were wet, or cold or hungry, or all three; and some of the time you'd go to sleep in the mud some place wondering if you'd wake up all together right there or scattered apart some place else; but you managed to get a laugh now and then just the same.

could read German got a laugh out of it, for every word was printed in German! It took the Boche just three years to find out that his efforts were not being appreciated as they should be and change the text of his remarks from German to English.

The Australian used to spend days trying to get their little aerial messages translated. When he succeeded he usu-

(Continued on page 31)

A lump of sugar is delivered at the home of Mr. Binks, the multi-millionaire.

THE EDITORIAL PC.

POLICIES—NOT POLITICS

Congress May Now Proceed

CONGRESS has said that it awaited the action of The American Legion before passing on a number of enactments of major importance to the country. It need wait no longer. If The American Legion in its months of organization had left the slightest doubt in any receptive mind of its attitude on the subject of deporting undesirable alien agitators and first-paper slackers, there can be no excuse for further doubt on that score. The Legion, by its majority voice, demanded immediate action on this score.

The Legion gave Congress the benefits of its advice upon the matter of a proper military policy for the United States. It rendered in detail its opinions upon proper beneficial legislation for men formerly in service. It defined a code of Americanism which should be of value to legislators in passing upon measures entirely outside the 1,001 pending measures concerning men and women who served in the world war.

One bit of information, however, the Legion did not impart to Congress. That was the terms of a readjustment of back pay for military service. Legion members feel that Congress rather adroitly passed the buck to soldiers on this so-called bonus question. If so, the Legion passed it right back by refusing to demand such an adjustment and fix the terms. Congress must pass upon this subject in the light of its own sense of fairness and equity. These qualities, we suspect, must be present in any enactment that will satisfy the majority of the country.

At any rate the united men and women who were in service have preserved intact that peculiarly fine and satisfying sense of self-respect that is the greatest reward of having been in service during the war.

Mental Defectives

ANALYSIS of the acts of so-called anarchists and Reds in the United States leads to the ready conclusion that these creatures are in reality sufferers from some virulent form of insanity, The mad viciousness of a recent attack by Red agitators upon an Armistice Day parade which resulted in the death of four veterans was merely an active expression of what this type of agitator customarily expounds from the soap box. It was the transition from raving maniac to homicidal mania.

The country should accept responsibility for such few of these defectives as owe their origin to our own soil. It should place them under restraint and proper medical attention when their insanity manifests itself by rabid utterances against freedom and democracy. It should not wait until the mental disease reaches a more dangerous stage and becomes a menace to individuals and property.

But the country owes no such responsibility to such of these defectives as come from alien sources. It should go no further than to restrain them at the first manifestations of these mental disorders and ship them forthwith to the land of their origin for such treatment as that land may happen to provide.

We fear that social investigators and students have been dealing too long with a problem that properly belongs to the alienists.

Adoption of the Weekly

THE AMERICAN LEGION WEEKLY has been established as a cooperative magazine, the ownership of which reposes in the members of The American Legion. While this had been done tentatively by the temporary organization it was done permanently by the Minneapolis convention, which gave the publication an earnest indorsement, and with a majority vote made every member of The American Legion an annual subscriber and part owner. The minimum rate under which the magazine can hope to exist was fixed by the delegates at $1 per year to each member, and this was entered into the Constitution of the Legion.

The policy of THE AMERICAN LEGION WEEKLY is found in the actions of the convention. These provided a definite and progressive policy affecting not only the unselfish interests of the men and women who were in service but of the majority of Americans. The magazine will continue to appear weekly and in its present form. It will be sent to every bona fide Legion subscriber as rapidly as the names of members can be added to the mailing list.

In many respects the WEEKLY is unique as a national publication. Its subscription growth from 12,-000 in its initial issue a few months ago to more than 300,000 in the current issue is without precedent. Its total circulation will shortly pass the half million mark. It will not be surprising if the million-mark is passed before the next convention. Such strides will establish a hitherto unthought-of precedent. In fact the WEEKLY is without precedent as a national magazine, even as the Legion is without precedent among great national organizations.

A Charted Course

THE bigness and soundness of The American Legion, as revealed through its charter convention, has been recognized generally by the press of the country. Editors the country over continue to find inspiration for stirring editorial matter in the Legion's initial expressions.

The Legion stands accredited by the country with having rightly interpreted the inevitable new order of things in America growing out of the country's common experience in the war. A greater service is yet to be given. In speaking its mind the Legion did not merely set up a code of conduct. It charted a course. Its members will follow that course to the end of the journey. They will not rest until the ideals of conduct and government they have adopted are no longer spoken of as ideals, by reason of having become accepted rules and simple circumstances of every-day existence.

Scenes of Yesterday

The flare.

Painted by Harvey Dunn.

The road to Essey.

Painted by J. Andre Smith.

Prince—of Wales and Good Fellows

England's Heir Apparent
Is a Regular

By
WILLIAM C. RICHARDS

THE Prince of Wales is "safe for democracy."

The royal special, a train of monarchical luxury which bears more marks of royalty than the heir-apparent to empire who rides on it, was ready to leap out of Windsor, Ont., the other day. Private Tim Murphy, late of the Canadian Ninety-ninth Battalion, walked up to the observation platform. Murphy had an idea which, to his way of thinking, was going to flabbergast the boy on whom some day will fall the ermine of Britain.

"You call yourself democratic, eh?" he began.

Edward Albert Andrew Patrick David Wettin, which is the name the prince can use when his breath is good, laughed.

"I hope I am," said he.

"Then gimme two bits," said Murphy, and waited for the crash.

His Royal Highness was clearly puzzled.

"What is it?" he asked.

"It's a bob, Your Highness, in the old country."

The prince did some excavating. He placed in Murphy's hand a Canadian twenty-five cent piece.

"And I know," he remarked, "that you can't get better than two per cent, old buddy, in this arid home-place of ours."

Two thousand voices roared their delight. Murphy held the silver high for all the Dominion to see.

"You're a brick, I say," he praised. The din of the mob multiplied. "Now," the soldier said, with all the irreverent gall of a top-sergeant, "give us a speech."

The Prince of Wales, whose interest in silk hats and pearl-buttoned shirt bosoms and silk-stockings is perfunctory in comparison with his attachment for the man with the symbol of service in the Great War at his button-hole, leaned over the vestibule rail.

"Only this: I don't want you fellows, in particular, to remember me as a prince, but as a comrade." The wheels began to grind. "So long, Canadians," he yelled. "Y-e-a, Prince," they bellowed back. The tracks unrolled between them, but until that animated line lost individuality and seemed but a brown canvas blown by the wind, His Royal Highness, the Prince of Wales, K. G., M. C., stood unhatted, waving his good-bye.

Why, I considered, as the hour neared of my presentation to him, had I not given more study to courtly custom? I knew Spalding's baseball guide and some now useless mathematics about the footage of a baseball field and the value of a field goal. I had even met the Queensbury manual, and from devious sources I had learned what to do with any number of forks up to four. What futile knowledge now.

Mind forayed for precedent. My royal intimates, it now seemed, were

Royalty carries with it the picture of dignity, majesty, pomp and aloofness. But that isn't the picture of the Prince of Wales America has seen. Mr. Richards's story is a "close-up" of a young man who rolls his own, likes American jazz and American girls, and hates to get up in the morning. It is a story of the youth as he is today, which gives an unusual insight into what the king of tomorrow will be.

restricted to the puppet princes of the plays, Kings Lear and Baggot, the Earl of Pawtucket, the Sultan of Sulu, Yetive of Graustark, Shine-Ball King Cicotte and Ban Johnson, the celebrated czar. The Sultan of Sulu, as a pattern, offered one terrifying obstacle. As I recalled, after the populace had sung, "Hail to the king; this is a joyous day," or some such lyrical delight, I had a vague remembrance of villagers breaking into a Texas Tommy.

Now I would no more think of Texas Tommying than I would envisage Irvin Cobb as a dancing partner of Pavlowa or William Howard Taft standing on tip-toe in gauze drapes and plunging through paper hoops astride a circus horse, or Mr. Bryan getting crocked.

ONCE in and introduced, moreover, I would be conversationally stymied. I might start with captious reference, possibly, to the late bereavement of Charles Comiskey, of Chicago, Ill. One cannot talk housing conditions, the most timely subject, to a person whose home suggests the Biltmore and the Commodore and

the Ritz welded in one, and with not a single bed which spends its daytime idleness hooked to a door.

I took comfort from an incident of the day previous. There had been an hour's stop at an Indian reservation. The prince had added to his endless appendages. He became Chief Morningstar. The christening over, an old chief gussied up in beads and paint, given an exotic touch by the pair of rubbers in which he shuffled, put his arm about the prince's waist and two-stepped about the ring. When it was halted, a string of Sioux issued. Then a salaam, a gorgeous thing that looked as if it might back-fire, but didn't. The prince went to American slang for help.

"Atta boy," he said.

It eased my mind some. I moved with more confidence along the line to the introduction.

"How do you do, Your Highness," I said, and wondered whether the official scorer would give me a hit or an error.

My right hand met his left.

"Got to do it," he excused the southpawing. "They nearly shook my right hand off in Toronto."

Behind me was a Canadian doughboy, quite red about the ears and in the grasp of a great embarrassment. One hand was bandaged.

"Where?" the Prince asked.

"Cambrai."

"Quite a tiff, too." Frock-coated gentlemen behind the soldier looked their impatience. The prince didn't mind. A prince doesn't have to. The Prince of Wales drew the arm of the Canadian private through his. Suddenly there was a hurried fumbling at the royal pockets. His Highness frowned.

"Got a cigarette?" he pleaded.

The soldier's cheeks had the hue of Britain's flag.

"I've got the makin's," he stammered.

"Quite so. Very good." The prince held out a hand.

And then he who is to inherit the purple rolled a cigarette. He handed back the bag and the papers. "Let me see you again, won't you," he said to the speechless veteran, and turned to the formalities. Henry Ford was one of those who waited.

GEORGE V's son is a regular. He has the *bonhomie* of a Broadway John, smokes all day, admires a pretty face with an open affection, is bored by Beethoven, is a disciple of American jazz, and he hates to get up early in the morning. Newspaper men on the train frothed a bit over the fancy for feminine beauty of the next head of the House of Windsor.

"He's stuck me a couple of times," a representative of a world famous news bureau told me. "There was a girl I was interested in a bit at Lake Louise, an

(Continued on page 30)

Few good shots are born. Practice will tell the tale.

Changing the Target

Doughboy Must Vary War's Style to Hunt Big Game

By L. L. LITTLE

IT IS reported that many old hunters who were sure shots were disappointed and even disgruntled because the War Department did not become enthusiastic over their offers to teach soldiers how to shoot. It is certain that a far larger number of ex-soldiers who did learn to shoot on the range or in actual warfare are due for even greater disappointment when they make their first attempt at big game.

Just as the War Department ruled, and rightly, that just any old method of shooting, self-learned, would not do for the training of our recruits, so the highly technical and scientific range shooting we learned from the Army will not fill the bill for us as we turn to sport shooting. The elements are the same, for the chief desire is to put a bullet in a particular place. Some millions of us learned a lot about cones of fire, grazing shots, ricochets, sighting shots, and danger zone. These mean little to the sportsman except as theory and, be it said, far less to the game itself. Our big game, for some reason, has never been trained to expect and await sighting shots, but its understanding of the danger zone is complete. To a moose, the danger zone is a place to get away from with the utmost speed.

Instead of the staccato voice of the officer or observer, giving distance, setting of sights, direction and target, the sportsman who finds his first deer may hear a rustle of twigs, the swish of branches returning to their accustomed places, and he may get a fleeting glimpse of an object moving directly away from him or crossing his front at any angle, headed either to right or left. At the best, he may have a warning whisper from a guide, after which he may see a great moose standing broadside at an uncertain distance for a still more uncertain time. There may be time to set sights and there may not.

The wisest thing to do is to pull a bead and fire, for game is as nervous as the service rifle seemed to be when you first shot for record with a coach beside you. Assuming that there is time to judge distance and set your sights accordingly, the chances are very high that the "enemy" will disappear hurriedly. You missed your big chance and that is the end of it.

Another occurrence, just as frequent with the beginner, is the so-called "buck fever." In this case, the chaffing received does not allow even the relief afforded by swearing; having lost your nerve at sight of the animal, you haven't even enough left for expression. About the only comfort one has after an attack of buck fever is to be gained from reading what Colonel S. W. Brookhard, U. S. A., once said about it: "Everybody has it; that is, everybody with any brains. A bonehead might be exempt. It is the anxiety or fear of failure that enters every appreciative mind at the beginning of any new undertaking."

AT THE Small Arms Firing School, every class is told how buck fever once attacked one General Bates and how he overcame it. The general says that he went out anxious to make a good showing and confident that he would do so. As he approached the deer country, he carried his rifle ready and up near a port arms. He was expecting to see a deer at any moment and still he did not exactly expect it at the moment when it did jump.

There it stood, full broadside, and only sixty or seventy yards away. It would not stand long, but it was a beautiful shot, and the achievement of his first deer crowded all else out of his mind for the moment. He tried to lower the rifle, but it would not come down. He pulled on it, swung his weight on it, and still it did not respond. The deer ran away and he never did fire at it. The thing happened and it did not happen. The deer was there all right, but the general did not pull down on his rifle—he pushed up. He was controlled by a mental illusion. But he was not ashamed of it and cured himself by telling it as a joke on himself. It did not happen again.

As a matter of fact, there are three principal possibilities of error: the rifle, the ammunition, and man himself. Mechanically, the first two may be dismissed. Practice with the weapon until the owner knows all its peculiarities, if it have any, will care for the first. The manufacturers make ammunition fitted for every purpose, and man has but to choose that which is best fitted for the rifle he uses and the purpose he has in view. Of the errors of man, there are also three cardinal ones: the eye, flinching, and buck fever. For the beginner, the greatest of these is buck fever. As practice continues, the error of the eye becomes the most important. Flinching may be dismissed for the present purposes, it being assumed that those who have done

Shoot on the range until you can assume a natural position immediately

range work have been cured of that.

With the fever out of the way as shown by General Bates's experience, the one really important thing is the eye in its quick judgment of distance. There will always be some error there. Certainly, few men can say positively that the range is .200 yards rather than 250. If you lost your one big chance as suggested above, the chances are that the rifle was not at fault, nor was the ammunition.

Here, then, comes the question of trajectory, which, in the Army, is for someone else to figure out and then give the results. In the field, your guide cares little about telling you of trajectory; and the probability is that he would not know what it meant if you mentioned it. Without attempting to be technical, let it be said that a bullet travels through a curved path between the muzzle of the gun and its target. It is this that we mean as we speak of trajectory. If you missed that moose, although you held steadily, it can be explained by the fact that you misjudged the distance and that had you had a low velocity bullet. That is, in order to shoot 250 yards, the bullet had to travel very high during part of its course.

Manufacturers can overcome this by increasing the velocity of the bullet, flattening out the curved path it takes, and therefore greatly increasing the distance in which the bullet will hit a mark of given height. Clearly, this will atone to a large degree for your error of distance. To use military parlance, it "increases the danger zone." If this can be done without sacrificing accuracy, much of the difficulty is gone.

IT is needless, surely, to enlarge upon the difficulty of judging distance. If you have not learned it from the common experience of guessing whenever out on a hike, you will find it fully laid out in any standard treatment of rifles, or in the War Department's books upon musketry. It is hard enough when there is time for examining fence posts, telegraph poles, stumps, rocks, or anything which happens to lie between you and the object being discussed. When it must be judged in a fraction of time without taking the eye away from the animal, it becomes too difficult for words to state accurately. When, in connection with the curved path of a bullet, one realizes that a deer at broadside offers a target (for killing purposes) of about three inches about the heart, the whole thing becomes extremely simple.

Misjudge the distance by fifty or seventy-five yards, and the bullet, striking where it was aimed, will only maim, not kill. If the trajectory is flat enough, you

probably will have a nice load on your back and a fine head for your den. Suppose, for instance, that you have low velocity ammunition and your sights set for 200 yards. Pick up a deer at 100 yards, without time to reset your sights. A mid-range error (or height of trajectory) of five inches will place the bullet quite too high for the purpose. Let the target be of approximately eight inches, such as a moose offers, and if you have a 3,000-foot velocity, a mid-range error of this same five inches should be the maximum at 300 yards.

A solution sometimes offered is that of using a fine or coarse sighting, depending upon whether you think the distance less or more than that for which you have placed your sights. This is generally regarded as inadvisable, for the amount is hard to judge. A coarse sight causes the front sight to hide much of the animal, and one will almost automatically lower. Horace Kephart solves it by carrying a rule in his head for the military rifle with a point blank of 150 yards. It is:

200 yards=3 inch drop.
225 yards=5 inch drop.
250 yards=8 inch drop.

He says he finds it far easier to carry the rule of three, five, eight in his head and to aim accordingly than to try to vary the amount of front sight which he can see.

The end and aim of all hunting, of course, is to kill as quickly and painlessly as possible. As a consequence of this, the old Maine guide's idea is rather generally accepted: i. e., hit him with the biggest possible chunk of lead. It is merciful and desirable, but it leads into all sorts of trouble. The bigger and heavier the bullet, the greater must be the charge of powder in order to avoid high trajectory, the heavier the gun, and the greater the recoil. None of these is desirable, and a mushroom bullet is the next solution offered. The sportsman does not wish a clean wound through the animal, with the exit little larger than the entrance, and the power of the bullet expended upon air beyond.

A small bullet of high velocity may do just this without inflicting a death wound. An extremely heavy bullet may strike the target at the right place, but its power is gone by the time it reaches the mark, the result being only a flesh wound, or a dead bullet lodged against a heavy bone. A light bullet at high velocity is likely to glance away from the skeleton. The bullet which bores a clean hole through bone without shattering it, or which comes to a stop upon striking such an obstacle, is equally undesirable. The happy solution is the one which will bore to some extent but will mushroom within

the body of the animal, expending its full shocking power where it is most needed.

When the velocity of the bullet is such as to prevent light tissues from giving way quickly enough, it shocks and bruises sufficiently to prevent an animal from going far. The ideal bullet for sporting purposes is one which will expand, not upon impact, but after a certain penetration, but still is heavy enough to prevent turning or a ricochet when striking the heavier bones. It goes without saying that it must be chosen with a view to particular size of game.

SOMETHING of position may not be out of place. Those most likely to be used are standing, kneeling, and prone. About all that can be said of the prone position for field work is to hope that luck is with you. As is true of all hunting, the man who approaches game while crawling must expect to sight his quarry at any moment, at any distance, and while he is in any position of torture or contortion. Trust to luck and blaze away; the target is but fleeting. It is fair to assume that the average American has learned to stand and deliver. If he has not, then the place to learn is the rifle range. There is only one rule in hunting: get the natural point and pull. Do not think of the right or the left elbow, the peculiar hunch of the left hip as a rest for elbow, the angle of feet, or trigger squeeze. Shoot on the range until you can assume a natural post immediately as by second nature. Then go after game.

The kneeling position seems to be the favorite American way. Probably two-thirds of the paintings made of pioneers, whether shooting Indians or game, have put the figure on one knee. It is easy and rapid to take, and for a hurried shot is second only to the prone for certainty and steadiness.

The whole problem of hunting comes back to this, that best results will come from a complete foundation in offhand shooting and in judging distances and conditions. It depends almost entirely upon the hunter. Few good shots are born. Practice, if you are as intelligent as Colonel Brookhart expects, will tell the tale. The rifle is a tool meant to put a bullet in a particular spot. If it is rightly chosen, the ammunition is what it should be, and you hold it correctly, it will fulfil its mission. Error is largely human, and therein lies the explanation of the nervous indigestion so frequently blamed upon shooting pieces.

Shoot when you see it. Better a miss than never to shoot at all.

The birds are singin' juist as sweetly here,
    The flowers are a' the same;
But wi' each warbled note, each noddin'
    bloom,
        Ma hairt turns hame.

The trees are gled wi' springtime, Mither
    mine,
    But I'm nae here the noo—
I'm wanderin' oot amang *oor* orchard
    trees,
        Wi' you.

Lines frae the
Rhein, 1919

The Rhein flaws sparklin' tae the sea; in
    dreams
    I float me doon alang
The magic path its shinin' waters trace,
    Swift miles an' lang.

Across the wide sea an' the fallow land,
    The mountains, too, a' past,
I gather ye intac ma eager arms—
    Back hame, at last!

Ah, haste the day! Ye've watchit lang
    an' true,
    Wi' greets, through weery nicht;
But noo the east is palin'; an' I come
    Wi' mornin's licht!

                                                —*John Fletcher Hall.*

Five Years and One Night

By ROBERT J. CASEY

TOM BRANCH was coming back. Every "sleigh-rider," "book peddler," "jabber," "hop-head," and "steam-guy" in the big city's bad lands knew of it through the unexplainable wireless of the under-world five minutes after the barred door of the penitentiary had clanged shut behind him. He was coming back, and there was to be a day of reckoning.

Ferell, police reporter for the *Chronicle*, encountered Branch by accident as he stepped from a train in the Union station. They exchanged greetings. "What are you going to do?" inquired the reporter.

"Kill a man," announced Branch with simple sincerity. "I'm going to kill Marvin Belknap at the earliest possible moment."

Ferell smiled incredulously. It was not customary, as his experience went, for men contemplating murder to talk about it.

"Wouldn't blame you particularly," he commented. "Do the community some good to be rid of him—but——"

Branch straightened his broad shoulders, raised an arm and studied the wrinkles that marked his coat for a product of the prison workshop.

"I've been five years in stir, Ferell," he said. "Five years paying for a dead horse that I didn't kill. And I'm going to square accounts."

Ferell was silent for a moment. He remembered the case—old Marvin Belknap, a millionaire drug importer, suddenly brought to book as a potent factor in the city's cocaine traffic, had found himself facing a term in a federal penitentiary. With a craft worthy of him he had suddenly shifted the responsibility to the shoulders of a subordinate. Tom Branch had gone to Leavenworth and had acquired the dubious accomplishment of manufacturing brooms.

Ferell often had looked forward to this occasion. He had believed Branch innocent. And he had known that five lost years would be charged against the account of Marvin Belknap with compound interest he could never pay.

"There's no use in it, Branch," he counselled. "You can't get away with murder. The law doesn't make any distinction between sheep and goats. You should be given a medal to encourage you to shoot the old sinner—but you won't be."

"Perhaps not, but it's going to be worth the price. Inside the law or outside of it, I'm going to collect."

BRANCH passed on out through the smoky trainshed and half ventilated waiting room to the street and stood for a moment watching the passing traffic. The frosty evening air had the tang of sulphur in it, and the squalor of the slums had set its mark upon the dingy buildings across the street—the stream of workers which threatened to engulf him was a backwash from the city's life, drab, mud-tinged, short-current, colorless, unbeautiful. But his heart warmed unaccountably as he watched it surge under the ghastly flicker of the arcs.

Wretched, unromantic, unlovely as these folks were, they were his own people—honest seekers for a meager living—elemental animals, but very likely possessed of an elemental animal's vices and virtues, incapable of lasting friendships, unable to betray.

He breathed deeply, welcoming the coal-laden vapors as an antidote to the prison air that still seemed to fill the recesses of his lungs. His city!—five years of wasted life could not change that. The sense of free living was his again and made him feel more poignantly how great had been his loss.

He walked across the bridge into the great heart of the city and felt the thrill of the discoverer in watching the dancing pools of colored light where electric signs cast their reflections upon the water, knowing anew the power of unfettered action as the rush of the evening traffic swept past him.

.   .   .   .   .

Marvin Belknap lived in a house that matched his soul—a great, gray-stone mansion that stood in a park of gaunt, leafless trees, silent and alone—a dead cell in the eager life of the north shore district that surrounded it. From this watch-tower on the heights, Marvin Belknap directed his puppets in the mills that fed the police courts—beyond reach of his victims—above the law.

At the corner a taxicab was waiting. "Get in," ordered the woman.

Belknap was a power in the community with an influence doubly potent because of the half-defined fear that accompanied it. His wealth was indisputable, his social standing unassailable, and his shameless lack of morals an axiom among his neighbors. But for all his sinister significance in the community, Marvin Belknap was not master of himself.

THE word that had been passed through the drugged haunts of the under-world reached him early in its course. He knew as certainly as the police that Tom Branch was on his way home. He knew as surely as the gun-men of the slums, whose hands made their own vengeance, that a reckoning was close at hand.

He sat at his desk in his marble walled study built into the tower at the corner of his gray house and confessed to himself that, in electing Branch to be the scapegoat for his adventures in the cocaine industry, he had been guilty of a serious misstep. The judge had betrayed his trust when he sentenced the young man to five years at hard labor when the maximum term was ten. And the police—tools of an administration which had received no campaign assistance from Mr. Belknap—were strangely apathetic when he asked that protection be furnished him. Time enough, the chief had told him, to post a guard when there were actual signs of danger.

He took an automatic from his desk drawer, slipped in a loaded clip, pulled back the slide, set the safety catch and replaced the pistol where it would be near his hand. There was some satisfaction, he thought, as he surveyed his surroundings, in the strength of the marble walls. They followed the curve of the tower except for a semicircular niche to the left of the door where stood a bronze cast statue of winged victory. It was a large statue. The niche was perhaps three feet across and more than two feet in depth. But otherwise the contour of the room was unbroken. Its one window could be fitted with iron shutters in a day or two and then—he smiled with assurance—then he would have little to fear from Tom Branch..

Branch hailed a taxicab—a luxury as strange to him now as the prison hardships had seemed five years ago. He lay back in the cushions watching the city slip by in the lamplight and shadow. Through park and residence district the car sped aimlessly, and Branch felt that he had never been more hopelessly alone. Homes—these brilliantly lighted apartment buildings were homes—places where human beings lived as God had ordained that humans should live. Homes! Places that by their very nature were closed to him—a prison bird. All the pent bitterness of the endless days and nights behind iron bars surged over him. He was measuring the value of five years by the standard of the hopeless hours he was living now.

THERE was a broad veranda around three sides of the Belknap mansion— a shadowy place far from the searching flicker of the corner arc-lamp. To the right side of the house a number of trellises, so gray, weather roughened and empty that it took quite a trick of the imagination to connect them with flowers, stretched up to the overhanging eaves. Branch, who had made his way to the house in the protecting shadow of a conveniently located stone wall, grasped the ladder-like rungs and swung up over the porch rail with ease.

Instantly he dropped flat in the blackness. A plain-clothes man sauntered by with the artful aimlessness that is the professional detective's chief distinguishing mark. He looked toward the house with an eloquent casualness that caused Branch to review quickly the circumstances of his coming. He was convinced that no policeman or casual pedestrian had seen him in the last three blocks of his journey, but he felt suddenly uneasy. He lay concealed in the dark several minutes after the detective had crossed the street and disappeared. Then he arose suddenly, clinging to the shadows as he skirted the house toward the front door.

He knew his ground. He had been over every inch of the house dozens of times before when society gossip had mentioned him as an eligible suitor for the hand of Mary Knight, Belknap's ward. That was yesterday . . . —or a thousand years ago.

The door was worth a trial. Failing to effect an entrance there he would have better luck, he knew, at the French windows of the conservatory on the opposite side of the house.

Still watching the street for a sign of further inquisitive activity on the part of the detective, he moved on, his back flat against the wall. Perfunctorily he turned the knob and pushed gently. His breath stopped with an involuntary catch. The door was unlocked and swinging inward. It seemed that the balance of fortune had turned, and he did not stop to question it. A second later he was in the long hallway, listening to the singing of the radiators and breathing in the welcome warmth of the house. He could see down the long corridor through an open door into a lighted room. His heart thumped expectantly as his eye caught the gleam of white warble. Before him lay Marvin Belknap's study. His quest was nearing its end.

Stealthily he crept toward the tower room.

SUDDENLY came catastrophe.
A shot echoed through the pent hallway like the blast of a cannon. He caught a glimpse of a moving shadow and almost simultaneously a familiar figure lurched into view in the rectangle of light that marked the study entrance. It was Marvin Belknap. He held a pistol in his right hand and his face was twitching in the throes of death. He pitched forward across the threshold.

Without hesitation, Branch opened the door part way and, crouching low to prevent his appearing in silhouette in the vision of a possible policeman, moved quickly on to the porch again.

Deliberate caution was sacrificed almost immediately to the necessity for speed. A police whistle shrilled in the street and a formidable barrier to escape in

Those five lost years would be charged against the account of Melvin Belknap.

that direction bulked large in the shape of the detective he had noticed a few minutes before. Pressing close to the wall he ran to the other side of the house. He turned the corner intent upon the danger behind him, came almost abreast of the French windows before he was aware of it, and suddenly realized that

he was not alone. Something was moving just in front of him—intangible, uncanny, but horribly real. He caught a faint odor of perfume and doubted his senses. A woman! Preposterous!

Almost simultaneously he remembered that a faint light from the French windows, while too dim to bring him to the attention of a watcher in the street, was none the less sufficient to make him the easy victim of the person ahead. He took a step toward the rail. Then a voice brought him up short like the snapping of a whip about his ears.

"Move straight ahead," came a tense whisper. "I am armed and shan't hesitate to shoot." Without questioning the command, Branch obeyed it. Nothing was to be gained by entering into a controversy which might delay him until the detective could reach the house from the street. For some reason which he did not attempt to analyze, this other person did not plan his immediate denunciation. He passed swiftly before the tall glass doors and became conscious of rapid, irregular breathing, very close to him, and an increased prevalence of the elusive scent.

"You will go on to the end of the porch, down the steps to the *porte cochere*," came the whisper. "Then along the drive and through the garage. I'll give you more instructions when you get there. And don't make a false step." The cool menace in the order was obvious.

"I understand," he said. There was something sinister in his guide's assumption that he knew his way about the Belknap premises well enough to carry out her directions. But in view of the other surprises of this amazing night it was little enough to puzzle over. He moved swiftly toward the *porte cochere* and heard vaguely the movement of skirts behind him.

A MOTORCYCLE had stopped at the curb before the house and a number of voices were blending in an excited chorus. He did not need the menace of a pistol at his back to speed his steps. A few seconds later he had descended two steps at a time from the velvet night of the veranda to the more penetrable darkness of a tree-arched driveway. He ran along the grassy edge and noted in his wake the sound of footsteps so light and quick he scarcely could distinguish them from the beating of his own heart.

The garage door was open. He passed through the building to a second door, swung it outward and stood in a cemented alleyway. Perhaps two seconds later the figure glided through the opening.

"North," she breathed. "Through the hedge behind Martin's garage. Then north again through the arbor and out over the wall to that little grove at Linden and the Lake road —and hurry."

At the corner a taxicab was waiting— the motor running and the chauffeur alert.

"Get in," ordered the woman, stepping momentarily from the enshrouding gloom into the dim light of a street lamp.

A shot echoed through the hallway. A familiar figure lurched into view. It was Marvin Belknap, his face twitching in the throes of death.

Branch caught his breath unbelievingly. He had identified her and felt suddenly numb at the thought of the situation. The flickering light had shown a wisp of coppery hair protruding from under a close-fitting hat, a straight nose and a determined little chin—a face that had not lost its wistful beauty in five years. The girl was Mary Knight—ward of the man who lay dead on the threshold of the tower room.

He gave no sign of recognition, but stepped quickly to the cab and entered it. His ready acquiescence threw the girl off her guard. She followed him into the car, just as it darted away from the curb, and was thrown against the door frame by the jerk as the clutch engaged. Before she could regain her equilibrium he had seized her right wrist.

The struggle was brief. She dropped the pistol with an angry sob, but made no outcry as he recovered it and forced her back into the seat.

"It's safer this way, Mary," he told her. All resistance ceased at the mention of her name.

"I thought I might be spared this humiliation," she answered in a voice harsh with suppressed rage and chagrin. "But no matter—what do you intend to do with me?"

"What had you intended to do with *me?*"

The girl hesitated a moment as the taxi, which had gotten well under way, swung around the corner into the drive and sped cityward.

"I should have killed you," she said tensely, "as you killed him—in cold blood."

"So that was the way of it. . . . I was to have been sacrificed again. This time to save you!"

"I?"

"Who else? I was there. I heard the shot. I saw him fall. I find you with a pistol in your hand. . . . How can you deny it?"

Rage choked her reply into halting, incoherent bits.

"You dare— You accuse me—you— ingrate—murderer of old men."

Her vehemence surprised him.

"You act it well, Mary," he conceded. "But unfortunately I saw. There was a

(Continued on page 24)

B U R S T S *and* D U D S

In the early days of the war mud was believed by some soldiers to be good for sore feet. After a long, forced march one Tommy was seen bathing his tired feet in the mud when another caught sight of him.

"Hi, you," he shouted, "get your dirty feet out o' that mud! Don't yer know we got ter sleep in it tonight?"

Two doughboys leaning moodily over the rail of a transport three hundred miles at sea watched a tiny fishing schooner tossing on the waves.

"Must be old fishermen in that boat," remarked the man from Massachusetts.

"You s a i d a mouthful, bo,"agreed the one from Oklahoma. "If they ain't, they darned well will be before they reach land in that thing."

There was a Medical Corps man who gave his patients a pill no matter what the ailment. One day a big burly army chauffeur came in and complained of a sore knee. The M. D. promptly gave him a tiny white pill. The big fellow swallowed it and then started to shake his leg vigorously.

"What are you doing that for?" asked the M. D.

"I'm trying to shake that pill down to my knee, Doc," answered the chauffeur.

The mayor of a certain village was very ill. At certain hours the doctors posted bulletins outside his house. At one c'clock the bulletin read: "Mayor very low." Three hours later came this: "mayor has only few hours to live." And then the last: "Eight o'clock; mayor has passed away."

Beneath this last bulletin a cynical politician w r o t e : "Nine o'clock; great alarm in Heaven; mayor has not arrived yet."

The American Legion Weekly will use jokes and pay for those that are acceptable. For the best received before Friday each week, not exceeding fifty words, five dollars will be paid; for the second best, three dollars; for all jokes accepted, one dollar. Manuscripts will not be returned. This offer is limited to those eligible to membership in the Legion.

The prize winners last week were: Joseph P. Reddy, New York City; Norman J. Whitney, Boston; Harry H. Dees, Mount Vernon, N. Y.; W. J. Gwinn, Pigeon, Mich.; Wm. P. Sherman, Connellsville, Pa.; Douglas M. Clarke, Springfield, Mass.; Fred C. Burris, Harrisburg, Pa.; France Russel, Butte, Mont.; Tyler B. Veasey, Jeffersonville, Ind.; C. H. Oldham, Baltimore, Md.; J. A. Donahue, Wheeling, West Va.

An Englishman in Pittsburgh was buying a horse. The seller, by way of proving to him what a wonderful animal it was, said, "With this animal you can leave Pittsburgh at six in the evening and be in Youngstown at two in the morning."

"A stunning horse indeed," replied the Englishman, "but, don't you know, I jolly well can't use him. What the devil would I do in Youngstown at two a. m.?"

Old darky, to shiftless son: "I hearn tell you is married. Is you?"

Son, ingratiatingly: "I ain't sayin' I aint."

Old darky, severely: "I ain't ask you is you ain't; I ask you ain't you is."

A firing party was marching a spy out to be shot one morning along French roads that were actually muddier than usual.

"Ah," muttered the spy, "no one with any heart would march a man through this mud just before he dies."

"Blime, what's your kick?" exclaimed a Tommy, "it's us as have to walk back through it."

As the Thirty-fifth Division was preparing to leave the Foret de Haye for the Argonne a labor battalion of negroes was moving in. A lieutenant of the Thirty-fifth was preparing for the march, hanging about his person while a dozen negroes looked on. His Very pistol, with its big, bell-shaped muzzle, attracted the attention of the watchers.

"What's dat, lieu-.tenant?" asked one.

"That's a Very pistol," explained the officer.

"Huh. Got any bullets for it? Is them the bullets? Lawdy, suh, you suhtenly could clear up de money in a crap game wid dat lil' gun."

Aged Aunt, despondently: "Well, I shan't be a nuisance to you much longer."

Nephew, reassuringly: "Oh, don't talk like that, Auntie; I'm sure you will."—*Passing Show.*

"Got a goldfish, have you?"

"Yes, I never liked to live alone."—*Le Rire.*

"Where are you going," the teacher wrote on the board.

"J o h n n y , read that," she said. Johnny did so. Then the teacher added the question mark at the end of the sentence.

"Now read it, Johnny."

"Where are you going, little button hook," said Johnny.

Suggestion No. 100,006 for stimulating attendance at local post meetings: Why not fulfil our army ambitions and invite a bugler to cooperate?

The Old Gang 'Round the Corner

The old gang 'round the corner's back—
we called the roll last night,
And twenty-one of us stood up who helped
to win that fight.
The navy, air and two marines from over
Dudley Square,
The Twenty-sixth and Fifty-fifth were
represented there.
We're not the same cop-teasing lads as in
the old days, when
We left the corner, dull and bare, to be the
fighting men.

The old gang 'round the corner's back
with gaps within our ranks,
For several quiet pals of ours, who died as
fighting Yanks;
McCarthy in an air raid, Saint Mihiel
claimed Tim Hurst,
And Smith was cited posthumus at Bel-
leau with the First;
Young Norm McKay gave up a leg that
Argonne woods be won,
And Billy Stone cursed at retreat, and
died to save his gun.

The old gang 'round the corner's back—
there's not much more to tell;
A story here and there from those who
charged the heights of hell;
The submarine that Joe's ship sank, the
Albatross that fled,
When Cohen dove out of the sun and let
his tracers spread.
How Sands was bayoneted and Brogna
saved his pal;
That was a corking story, but they
wouldn't tell it all.

The old gang 'round the corner's back—
we called the roll last night,
And twenty-one of us stood up who helped
to win that fight.
The navy, air and two marines from over
Dudley Square,
The Twenty-sixth and Fifty-fifth were
represented there.
We're not the same cop-teasing lads as in
the old days, when
We left the corner, dull and bare, to be
the fighting men.

—HENRY GILLEN.

The Old Sea-Captain

His tales such magic wonder could unfold
Of cargoes shipped from far West
Indian ports,
And argosies fleet-winged to foreign
pòrts
With strange, smooth-sounding names
like molten gold.
One saw the Spanish Main's dark pirates
bold;
And moon-lit battles on grim, narrow
decks;
And great sea serpents, and aban-
doned wrecks;
And treasure filched from some deep-
sunken hold.

He brought us teakwood inlaid with gray
pearl;
Carved toys of coral, jade and ivory;
Quaint wooden idols; flasks shaped like
a girl,.
From Java; spices, perfumes, tea.
But best, his yarns, that bore us all the
way
From snowy school days to sun-steeped
Cathay.

—CHARLOTTE BECKER.

Elegy Written in a Coal Bin

The furnace fire tolls the knell of falling
steam,
The coal supply is virtually done,
And at this price, indeed, it does not seem
As though we could afford another ton.

Now fades the glossy, cherished anthra-
cite,
The radiators lose their temperature,
How ill avail, on such a frosty night
The short and simple flannels of the
.poor.

—PERSONALITY.

Did it ever happen to you?

BULLETIN BOARD

Congress is investigating charges of waste of time and money in building army camps. One team foreman of A. Bentley & Sons and D. W. McGrath Company testified that he was not permitted to work at full speed nor even at normal speed. He declares he was called into the contractor's office and told not to do so much but just to keep things looking all right with a big number of men on the payroll. One member of a contracting firm is said to have received $20 a day from the Government that paid the soldiers $1 a day.

The House Military Committee favors the enlistment in the Army in peace times of non-English speaking inhabitants of this country. Under present conditions, Indians who cannot speak or write English are the only illiterates admitted to the Army. But in the war, almost a quarter of the men who came into the service through the draft were unable to read or write English.

One thousand jobs, ranging in pay from $2.00 a day and board to $195 a month and board, are waiting for wearers of red chevrons at navy yards, ordnance plants, and arsenals. Those who want them should apply to the Recorder, Labor Board, United States Navy Yard at Charleston, S. C., Key West, Fla., Philadelphia, Pa., Portsmouth, N. H., or Puget Sound, Wash.

Interesting figures just issued by the Department of Commerce show that in the first nine months of this year our exports to South America were $111,500,000 greater than for the same period last year. Another thing in the department's report that rouses attention is the item of thirty-nine dollars for imports from Germany in September, 1918. What were these imports?

Up in Toronto the other day a discharged colonel went to an employment agency for a job. He found his former army orderly in charge of the bureau. Instead of asking for a job the colonel asked about the weather and beat a strategic retreat.

Pirates, says a press dispatch, seized the steamer *Maria*, bound from Novorossysk to Batum, and took fifty million rubles from the passengers. With which they probably went out and bought two drinks.

Any estimate of the number of rats in the United States, says a daily newspaper, must be pure guess. This will be surprising news to those who had believed that all rats were numbered and filed alphabetically.

The erstwhile famous Keeley Institute has gone out of business. Either there are no more drunken men to be cured or else the few who still have that failing cherish it too much to get rid of it.

Is nothing to be left as it is? Now anarchistic mathematicians assert that the law of gravitation and the hypothesis that light travels in a straight line are both false. May be; we can't answer for crooked light, but we know absolutely that the law of gravitation was on the job last night when we reached the top of the stairs in the dark and thought there was still another step up.

There were nearly five million real Americans in the service when war was on, but none has better claim to the name than Corporal George Miner, Winnebago Indian, 123rd Infantry. No, he didn't wear war paint and carry a tomahawk.

In 1910, says the New York *Evening Post*, a locomotive repair shop in Germany, where 417 laborers were in service, delivered 484 locomotives a week. After the armistice the numbers of workers increased to 1,187, but the number of locomotives repaired fell to 411. In April of this year there was a further increase of workers to 1,253, but the output of locomotives fell to 353.

The news from Chicago that porterhouse steak was sold at eighteen cents a pound by striking butchers is made more interesting by the accompanying statement that one such market made a profit of $574 the first day. If profit can be made by undercutting so far the regular prices, it may narrow the search for the elusive profiteer.

It is an annual puzzle to calculate the date of Thanksgiving Day, and yet the President always does it in his proclamation with no apparent effort. He would confer a favor on Americans if he told us the secret.

Rear Admiral Bradley A. Fiske's new book of his own life, "From Midshipman to Rear Admiral," is making quite a sensation in naval circles. It puts squarely up to Secretary Daniels many grave charges concerning unpreparedness which the Secretary seems bound to answer.

General Pershing's idea of our future military policy includes an army of about 275,000, backed by a reserve acquired through universal six months training of all boys of nineteen years of age. The War Department wants an army of 500,000.

The War Department has a list of 101 general officers to be retained under the 18,000-officers bill. The list includes two generals, Pershing and March, two lieutenant-generals, Liggett, and Bullard, and fifty-five major-generals, headed by Wood.

Men who are interested in engineering of all sorts will find use for the list of 1,000 technical books prepared by the American Library Association to help the ex-service man in finding his place after discharge. Write to the A. L. A. in Washington, D. C.

The House of Representatives is considering Senator Edge's bill to authorize the organization under federal banking laws of corporations to finance American exports. Such a scheme is declared to be necessary because so many foreign buyers cannot pay cash for their goods now.

Sausage workers are on strike. A man who employs them—workers, not sausages—says they are demanding $245 a week, which is a good deal, even for a maker of "franks." Apropos of nothing, $30,000 has just been paid for a prize hog.

Indicative of a hard winter, we are assured by experts that the skin is thick on the belly of the codfish. This is used as a warning that automobile owners should store their cars with care for the winter.

A Long Island automobile repairer is restoring the car that was used by the former Kaiser during the German retreat. The ultimate purchaser will find that the car has great speed.

German miners, recognizing the critical situation in Germany due to coal shortage, have voted to work extra hours seven days a week from now till March in order to increase production.

A bill to award decorations to the next of kin of soldiers fallen in battle has been reported favorably by the House Military Committee.

WHAT THE LOCAL POSTS ARE DOING

An interesting post is that formed on November 6, by more than five hundred former members of the crew of the transport *Leviathan* and named the Leviathan Post. It is a lively post, and, now that the organization, business and election of officers have been disposed of, doubtless will be heard from in the future.

One of the largest posts in North Dakota is Mathew Brew Post, at Dickinson. Recently the post was divided into two teams which raced each other for new members; then the losing team gave the winners and the new men a prairie-chicken banquet. Monthly smokers and dinners and frequent dances make the post prominent in the life of Dickinson.

Hobart, the home of Post 54 of the Indiana Branch, claims to have a larger percentage of available service men enrolled as members than any other post in the state, if not in the country. About 200 men entered the service from Hobart, and by November 127 were in the post. Any other posts to be heard from?

Post 26 in Philadelphia has the distinction of having members who are in active service with the Army, for some of them are still with the Army of Occupation. The 285 members gave a dance November 13, which brought in a useful increase to the treasury.

"There is a ring of real Americanism in the resolutions adopted by Youngstown (Ohio) Post No. 15 of the American Legion, declaring its flat enmity to the spirit of lawlessness and bolshevism. They speak with the authority of those who have been tried and not found wanting." This is press comment on the work of the Youngstown Post in the recent disorders in that town.

A gay winter is being planned by Ernest DeNault Robertson Post No. 14 of Jamestown, N. D. A dance with "chow" on Armistice Day proved such a success that the members are laying out dates for other celebrations, which are calculated to bring the membership up from 215 to 500.

Here is another post with an impressive claim to the biggest increase in membership due to an organized drive. Greenpoint Post No. 241, Brooklyn, N. Y., went from 51 to 365, an increase of 610 per cent. A useful expedient in this accomplishment was a three-minute speech delivered every night at the local theater by a Legion member.

Tulsa (Okla.) loyalists, not satisfied with

To transact American Legion business that called for quick action, William B. Follett, of Eugene, Ore., hopped to Portland on a DeHaviland bombing plane. The picture shows, from left to right, Dean Hayes of Portland, Lieut. E. C. Battan, who drove the plane, Follett, Edward J. Eivers, and Jerrold Owen of Portland.

passing resolutions to deport convicted aliens, have offered to finance the deportation of 300 of them. Provided the government has not the ready cash, Tulsa will provide it and will take in compensation surplus automobile trucks in the possession of the government.

There is some misunderstanding among the posts about this page of notes. To receive space in the WEEKLY they should reach us three weeks in advance of the date of publication. The WEEKLY is not a daily newspaper; it takes some time to print it. Therefore notices received November 20 for publication in the WEEKLY of November 28 cannot be used.

"Now I'm one of the boys. I'm proud to be a member," said Lieut. General Robert L. Bullard, former commander of the Second Army, when he joined Bothwell Kane Post at Forth Worth, Tex. That town is the home of the *Legionnaire*, the Texas monthly Legion paper.

Champaign Post No. 70, Creston, Iowa, has installed an office where all discharged service men may go to obtain information on compensation, back pay, travel allowance, and so forth.

A woman's auxiliary has been formed by the Golden Gate (Cal.) Post No. 40. The membership of this post is now close to 5,000. It is one of four San Francisco posts which have united to form a county committee for supervision of the interests of veterans in the neighborhood. The other posts are San Francisco Post No. 1, Irwin Post No. 93, and Randolph T. Zane Post No. 143.

Powder River Post No. 13, Buffalo, Wyo., is growing rapidly. Two of the state's delegates to Minneapolis, Millie Webber and Jean Van Dyke, came from this post.

The furnishings of the Red Cross

Canteen Hut at Williamsport, Pa., have been presented to Garret Cochran Post for use in its headquarters.

In connection with possible riot duty in the coal strike, McFarland Post No. 9, La Junta, Colo., notified the governor of the state that "there is no authority vested in any officer or board of The American Legion to call out or pledge the Legion or any part of it for military duty in any emergency." The post stated that while its members were true Americans and ready to defend American institutions, they would act as individuals, not as a part of the Legion.

Posts of Cook and Lake Counties, Illinois, exerted themselves in a great "Victory Reunion and Circus" in Chicago from November 8 to 16 inclusive. The official war pictures of the Illinois Division in action, entitled "From Hell to Victory," were the sensation of the celebration.

Not "more money and less work" but "he who will not work shall not eat" is the motto of Post 171 of Meservey, Iowa. This post has adopted resolutions condemning the agitation being carried on by alien labor leaders and disapproving the action of strikers who seek to usurp the powers of the government.

Here's a challenge for basket-ball teams. Post No. 40, Plymouth, Mass., has formed a team and wants to arrange games with any other Legion teams in the state. Write to Manager F. H. Denlevy, 191 Court St., Plymouth.

Yonkers (N. Y.) Post No. 7 has passed the 1,500 mark in its membership and is approaching 2,000. It is arranging a grand ball for January 16 which will be the event of the social season in Yonkers. This post keeps up interest by meeting once every week.

Jefferson Post, in Louisville, Ky., has won the first skirmish in its fight on disloyalty in its city. The People's Church, whose pastor's utterances on the war have been subject to severe criticism, has been forced to disband because of the pressure exerted by the post.

The Vermont branch of the Legion is seeking an apology from the state governor for a letter of his concerning shellshocked soldiers. In it were the words "the supply of men who are waiting for the government to serve them something on a silver platter exceeds the demand." The governor has said that the words did not convey his real meaning.

Five Years and One Night

(*Continued from page* 19)

time when you would have hesitated to call me a murderer. You shot the old reprobate. Why get excited about it? If you hadn't shot him I would have choked him to death. The world is better off without him."

AGAIN came a moment of quivering silence. Branch, glancing through the rear window, saw a headlight swing into the street in their wake just as the nervous stutter of a racing motor reached his ear. The police had taken the trail. The girl did not seem to have noticed it.

When she spoke again her voice was calm enough, but there was a note in it that she could not identify.

"It was because I did remember the old days, Tom, that I forgot my duty and tried to take you away from the police. I went to the house because I heard you had threatened to take his life. . . . I arrived too late."

"Where had you been?" he inquired skeptically.

"In my own apartment. I haven't lived with him since the day he perjured you into prison. Oh, Tom, why didn't you come to me before you planned to do this awful thing?"

"Pull over," he put in coldly. "I have average intelligence and very little sentiment. You killed old Marvin yourself and you are trying to hypnotize yourself into believing that I did it. After all, what's the difference? If we can shake off the cops until I get away, you can tell them anything you care to—won't hurt my reputation any."

And then she burst into tears.

"I can't stand it! I won't! she declared between sobs. "It's bad enough to have you a murderer—but a liar, a selfish, scheming, traitorous cheat—ugh—I hate you."

Before he could guess her intention she had thrust her head through the half-open panel of the door and screamed to the chauffeur to stop. He followed instructions to the letter, killing his engine with a sudden application of the brakes. Branch had time neither to expostulate with the woman nor force the driver to crank his motor again.

A motorcycle roared alongside and another character entered the drama, a policeman obviously impressed with the seriousness of the situation.

"Pull over," he ordered. "Stick your hands up and get out."

* * *

The usual disorder that follows the intrusion of the law was evident in the Belknap home when Branch, Mary Knight and the taxi-driver were escorted to the tower room by the motorcycle policeman—weeping servants; a bored ambulance surgeon; a hard-faced, heavy-jowled police lieutenant in uniform; a hard-faced, heavy-jowled police lieutenant in civilian clothes; two patrolmen; a thin, professional ascetic whose part in the piece was not immediately evident; and Ferell, police-reporter.

All of the assemblage, except the

surgeon, the uniformed lieutenant, the unidentified one and Ferell, were standing in a confused throng in the outer hallway. The others were grouped about the body of Marvin Belknap, stretched out on top of the desk for examination, as the prisoners entered.

The professorial person looked up in surprise. Ferell's face was enigmatic.

"I followed 'em away from here," the motorcycle policeman explained. "Saw one of 'em cross the porch and chased 'em about two miles south in the drive. I think they know something about this."

"I shouldn't wonder," the professorial person replied. "The man's done time —the girl is Belknap's adopted daughter."

Branch for the first time felt the chill of hopelessness. The ascetic, it came back to him in a rush of unpleasant memories, was John Knox of the Department of Justice.

"One of you," Knox said in a matter-of-fact tone, "killed Marvin Belknap. You threatened to do it, Branch."

Branch looked at the girl, who stood trembling against the wall as if on the verge of fainting.

"Yes," he confessed slowly, "I did it. I said I'd kill him. I did, and I'm not sorry. Do as you please about it."

Knox turned to the lieutenant.

"He's your man," he said. Then as one of the patrolmen approached Branch to take him away: "Too bad you didn't wait a while, Branch. I came here tonight to arrest Marvin under the Harrison act. He'd have been safe in Leavenworth in a month or two."

"HARD luck," sympathized the lieutenant. "That's what comes o' bein' too fast. Take him away, Joe."

But Joe did not carry out the order. The girl, summoning every atom of reserve strength, sprang forward.

"It's a lie," she declared, "I did it." The lieutenant was shocked out of his vast placidity. The federal agent appeared unimpressed—double confessions bored him without surprising him greatly.

He looked coolly toward the motorcycle policeman—unconsciously assuming the authority which the lieutenant seemed willing enough to concede to him.

"Where are the others that were taken from these people?" he inquired.

"Only one gat. Branch had it. It's on the table there." Knox, the lieutenant and Ferell pressed forward simultaneously to look at it.

"I guess that let's you out, lady," the investigator decided. "You'll have to go along with him, but I don't think any grand jury in the world would ever indict you for shooting a man without a weapon." Knox knew the tricks of his trade. He had discovered through expensive experience that a man tells much when his word is doubted.

"He took it away from me in the cab," she persisted desperately. "He hadn't any pistol of his own."

But the latter declaration was repeated

in a tone that indicated her own surprise that he hadn't and carried small weight.

SHE rambled on hysterically.
"I hated Marvin Belknap. I hated him—" She stopped short when she became suddenly aware that the government agent was no longer listening to her.

The surgeon was holding up for inspection the bullet that had caused Belknap's death. Knox and Ferell started involuntarily.

"Guess again, sister," Knox advised her. "That gun on the table's a .32. This bullet's a .45, blunt nose, steel jacket."

Ferell broke into the conversation for the first time.

"Belknap's gun? What kind was it?" "Forty-five." This reluctantly. "But don't get it into your head that this was a suicide. No man living could have reached around with his right hand and shot himself under the left floating rib unless he's a contortionist."

Farrell's obvious lack of concern at the announcement of the location of the wound was even more dramatic than the tenseness of his voice.

"It was no suicide," he agreed. "Neither was the old man shot by either of these folks.

"I'll bet my salary for a year I can call the trick without moving from this spot. Look at the statue beside the door."

"Yes," admitted Knox, "it's chipped." "Look behind the statue. If my guess is right you'll find a black mark, a little less than shoulder high, running all around the niche from the side where the wing is chipped to the other—a line like a pencil mark."

The federal agent scrutinized the marble walls of the semicircular depression. He faced about abruptly and studied the spot where the body had fallen, then turned back toward the statue again.

"I wonder if such a thing could be possible," he debated with himself. Again he examined the streak on the wall, and the skepticism in his expression turned to amazed conviction.

"You win," he conceded. "The evidence is here. Belknap fired. Bullet hit the statue, slowed up a bit and followed the curve of the niche around."

"And ricocheted off at the left side," finished Ferell, "and hit the old man. Looks like there's a certain amount of justice left in the world after all. He probably saw Branch in the hall and took a shot at him with a rotten aim. The flattened face of the bullet marks it for a ricochet."

"It does," agreed the lieutenant with visible relief. "You'll have to appear at the inquest tomorrow"—speaking to Branch and Mary Knight—"you're excused for the present."

But they didn't seem to hear him. They were looking at each other, and the memory of five wasted years was fading.

The Uncommon Bond

By HENRY D. LINDSLEY
First Past National Commander

HENRY D. Lindsley, the retiring national chairman of The American Legion, pronounced the Legion as inseparable with American affairs and gave his estimate of the accomplishments of the Minneapolis convention in his farewell address to the new National Executive Committee, which met in Minneapolis on November 13.

"I esteem it a privilege, comrades, that I should this morning see the first meeting of the new National Executive Committee," said Mr. Lindsley.

"There are some here to whom I have not expressed my appreciation for the services they have rendered to me personally while I have been head of The Legion, and particularly during this convention. To each and every one of you I now express this appreciation and wish to give you, before leaving, this message:

"The First Annual National Convention of The American Legion has just elected a National Commander who, from experience, is more competent, in my judgment, to direct the affairs of The American Legion during the coming year than any man in the United States. I say this without disparagement to the large number of Legionnaires who in the years to come will be national commanders of The American Legion.

► "During the past six months National Commander D'Olier, without any title other than member of the National Executive Committee, without any thought other than service, has labored night and day to make The American Legion what it is today. He has had, as you know, directly under him the state organizations, and the life of the national organization has depended, and will continue to depend, primarily on the state organizations. He did a very wonderful work; but, outside of and beyond the work itself, the spirit with which he from day to day met great problems was a constant inspiration to me. The biggest thing I can ask you for the good of the Legion is that you give National Commander D'Olier the same splendid support which, during the past six months, he has given me.

"I want to ask you, as you go to every part of the United States, to constantly remember that National Headquarters always needs your advice and cooperation. It is always an inspiration for the head of The American Legion to come in contact with members of the National Executive Committee and with all other Legionnaires. Every time you tell the National Commander what he can do that will make the Legion a greater force for good in American life, you not only are rendering a personal service to him, but you are rendering a service to the nation.

"I ASK you, my comrades, to carry with you from this convention a very solemn obligation to put the spirit of The American Legion, as it has been demonstrated throughout this convention, into the life of the United States. It is, without doubt, the greatest convention from the standpoint of national good that has occurred since the Civil War. It ties our country together with a bond such as has never been known before. It assures us and our children the benefits of constitutional government in the United States.

"I did not have the opportunity yesterday at the convention to express appreciation to the members of the committees who served at the convention for the wonderful work done by them. I ask you who were members of these committees to take the message from me to those who labored with you. No committees have worked more diligently and more effectively for our country than these committees.

"The resolutions that passed this convention are the most momentous in recent history. There is not the shadow of a doubt about this. No member of the Congress, in the Senate or in the House, will fail to read carefully every one of these resolutions and will refer to them again and again during the coming year and thereafter. And by what the convention has done, those in public life will largely determine their course; for while they know this is a non-political association, and will remain so, it has nevertheless set a standard for those occupying positions in the public life of this nation, and those who cannot live up to this standard, in either party, are going to be retired to private life.

"I did not intend, my comrades, to say as much as I have here today. I only wanted to express my personal admiration for our new National Commander; to ask you, in a way perhaps that he cannot, for that support which is so essential to his successful administration; to thank you for your loyalty and your friendship for me and to have you know there can never come to me in life anything that I shall hold dearer than the honors you have conferred upon me in this convention.

"These things, dear indeed today, will become sweeter and sweeter in the years to come. I hope that, year after year, you and I will meet face to face and again clasp hands, remembering this great convention and the things it did.

"If there should ever come a time when an attempt is made to inject into The American Legion selfish or political purposes, you will harken back to this convention and remember the standard it has set in our minds and in our hearts as the standard and the spirit of The American Legion. The living force of this convention must continue to be a benediction to The American Legion, which is now inseparably a part of our country."

National Commander D'Olier replied:

"This is the first time since I have been associated with Past Commander Lindsley that I have had to take exception to any statement made by him. I was only a willing worker at National Headquarters, and the Past Commander values my services more than they deserve."

LETTERS FROM READERS

From a Congressman

To the Editor: I would go much further than the Lufkin Bill, H. R. 9416, which would prohibit the issuance of naturalization for five years to alien shirks, and deport those who surrendered their first papers. My attitude is indicated by my bill, H. R. 1240, which I introduced to provide not only for deportation of dangerous interned aliens, but to provide for the deportation of all aliens, who, being otherwise qualified for military service, claimed and were granted exemption for the sole reason that they were aliens.

The duty of America in respect to undesirable aliens is clear and unescapable. Those who came to this land from foreign shores did so because they saw here in America far greater opportunities and advantages than were accorded them in their native lands. They came here to enjoy those privileges which were denied them in their own native countries. They found here equality of opportunity and splendid possibilities for social and economic development and betterment. They were in no wise discriminated against. The opportunities of education were theirs. They were accorded the full protection of the law—in one word, they enjoyed the same benefits, privileges, advantages and opportunities that the citizens of America have enjoyed.

And yet, notwithstanding this liberal and generous treatment on the part of America, her government and her people, many of these aliens have repaid America with the basest ingratitude and treachery.

There can be no dissenting opinion among Americans, who desire to protect our population from the cunning, intrigue and treachery of these aliens, that they are undesirable residents. The restrictions which the government placed on aliens during the trying period of the war were reasonable. They were born of necessity and of a prudent regard for the country's safety and self-preservation.

This hostile and ungrateful class that reaped the benefits of all opportunities and privileges, boldly disobeyed all orders and laws, defied this country which was their benefactor and, by their actions and violations of the various laws, gave aid and comfort to the enemies of America.

If America was not good enough for these aliens in times of war, it is then too good for them in times of peace. We have sufficient room here for aliens and immigrants who will obey our laws and respect our institutions. But we have no room for the wily agitators and active agents of our enemies.

We cannot tolerate them in our midst. We cannot allow them to remain here, spreading the seeds of discord and rebellion and spreading the doctrine of bolshevism, of anarchy, and of defiance of law and order and authority. Were they permitted to remain here, they would proceed in their nefarious work of destruction. They have demonstrated con-

clusively that they are not in sympathy with American ideals and American free institutions. They would undermine the structure of this Republic, which American manhood and womanhood, by generous and patriotic sacrifices, have preserved and perpetuated. They cannot attach any blame to anyone but themselves for the fate of deportation which they so richly deserve. Our gates must be closed and our ports must be sealed to these agitators and international destroyers of all that we hold dear.

> JOHN C. KLECZKA,
> *Congressman from Wisconsin.*
Washington, D. C.

Makes Readers Think Twice

To the Editor: Regarding THE AMERICAN LEGION WEEKLY, I want to say that I think the organization can be proud of its official publication. Both the editorials and the articles are eye-openers, the kind that make the readers think twice, and should promote an active and intelligent interest in the workings of this nation of ours. I have only one suggestion to make, and that is that the class of advertising matter be kept high.
Millbury, Mass. G. K. H.

Liveliest on the Market

To the Editor: Please enter my subscription to THE AMERICAN LEGION WEEKLY for one year. I am sure that among ex-service men it is the liveliest and best weekly on the market and I don't think the members of The American Legion could get along without it, in fact here is one that doesn't want to miss an issue and I know that that is the sentiment of our post here. I wish you all the success possible and I hope to see the day when The American Legion numbers 4,000,000 men and THE AMERICAN LEGION WEEKLY has that many subscribers.
> HARRY C. CRIM.
Fort Lauderdale, Fla.

Much Appreciated

To the Editor: I wish to compliment you on your splendid magazine. I assure you it is much appreciated by all ex-service men.
Eaton, Colo. CHARLES A. CARLON.

With a Kick

To the Editor: THE AMERICAN LEGION WEEKLY is surely a soldier's magazine with a kick. I am glad we have such a publication which reaches practically all of us who have so much in common as a result of our service. I wish to thank you personally and in behalf of all of the soldiers of the Missoula Post No. 27 for your able article, "What's Wrong with War Risk?" I believe you are performing a distinct service in going into this matter and explaining to the men that the continuance of the government insurance is the best business policy before them for consideration at this time. The magazine is bright, well edited, and contains the kind of stuff we like to read.
Missoula, Mont. D. D. RICHARDS.

The Cement

To the Editor: I enjoy THE AMERICAN LEGION WEEKLY and believe it is the cement that will hold the Legion members together.
Charter Oak, Iowa. C. J. TURNER.

"How Can You Do It?"

To the Editor: I read THE AMERICAN LEGION WEEKLY every week and think it is a great little WEEKLY, but I can't understand how you can put it on the market for a nickel. I hope it keeps up in the future the breezy news about us boys who served, as it has in the past.
Chicago, Ill. JOHNNY SCHIFF.

None Can Compare

To the Editor: I wish to congratulate you on the splendid showing made by THE AMERICAN LEGION WEEKLY. There is certainly no other magazine in circulation which can be compared with it from an ex-service man's viewpoint.
> FINLEY WHITE.
A. & M. College, Miss.

Admires the Spirit and Fight

To the Editor: I have been able to get almost every issue of THE AMERICAN LEGION WEEKLY and admire the spirit and good fight for the rights of the boys who stood together in the great war which the Legion is taking up. May the good work be continued.
> DAVID H. MOOR.
Los Angeles, Cal.

Interesting in Every Page

To the Editor: I am receiving my copy of THE AMERICAN LEGION WEEKLY and certainly find it interesting in every page. Allow me to congratulate you on your clever publication. I hope every one of us four million supposed to stick together, will be interested in your publication.
> THEODORE B. GEORGE.
Calgary, Alberta, Canada.

(*Continued on page 34*)

INFORMATION

The American Legion Weekly will undertake to answer in this column practical questions asked by readers affecting the interests of men who were in the service. Questions will be answered in the order of their receipt, except that precedence may be given now and then to questions of a wide general interest.

Military Decorations

To the Editor: Can you give me some information relative to the oak leaf worn on the Distinguished Service ribbon, also further information relative to the medals which were awarded in the A. E. F.?

New Orleans, La.   J. K. SLOAN.

The wearing of a Cluster on the Distinguished Service ribbon indicates that the recipient has twice won the distinction of the Distinguished Service Cross, as not more than one D. S. C. is ever given to an individual.

The Congressional Medal of Honor is authorized to commissioned officers or enlisted men for distinguished gallantry in action only. A number were issued during and since the Civil War. They were first distributed March 25, 1863. Although the law provides our Medal of Honor can be conferred on foreigners, the records show that none has been given. According to a ruling of the British Army, the Victoria Cross can be conferred only on a British subject.

The Distinguished Service Cross is given to any person "For extraordinary heroism in connection with military operations against an armed enemy." (Wording of law as of July 9, 1918.) The Distinguished Service Medal is awarded "For exceptionally meritorious service to the government in a position of great responsibility." The recipients of this medal, as also the Distinguished Service Cross, may be officers, enlisted men or civilians. Both of these medals were issued for the first time during the present war.

In addition to the badges and medals listed in circular from the Adjutant General's Office, Washington, D. C., dated March 15, 1919, including the three major decorations, namely: The Congressional Medal of Honor, the Distinguished Service Cross, and the Distinguished Service Medal, the new Victory Medal has been directed for issuance under G. O. 83, W. D., 1919. During its preparation of design and to take its place in a way, the Victory Button is being issued for wear only by honorably discharged soldiers.

A medal should be worn only on dress uniform or upon special military occasions. At other times in uniform, the ribbon is worn, indicating that the wearer has received the medal. The ribbon indicates possession of a medal for a particular campaign or service. All medals which are authorized for issue to enlisted men, including retired enlisted men, are issued free of charge.

The arrangement for the proper wearing of medals and ribbons is cited in S. R. 41, Changes No. 10. Those who are entitled to more than one ribbon should wear them so that the ribbon indicating the first campaign will be to the right, excepting in cases where the wearers possess a Congressional Medal of Honor, a Distinguished Service Medal or a Distinguished Service Cross, in which case the ribbon indicating same should always be placed to the right of the other ribbons, taking precedence in the order named.

Soldiers' Pay and Present Status of O. R. C.

To the Editor: Will you please inform me, through the columns of the WEEKLY, of the following: (1) Are all soldiers entitled to pay from the date of taking oath? The case in mind is that of a soldier who made application for aviation in May, 1917, was examined and took oath August 17, 1917, and ordered to report to Austin, Tex. (Ground School), November 3, 1917. (2) What is the status of the present Officers' Reserve Corps? When will they be called out for maneuvers and who will be called? Will every member of the reserve be called out when call is made? For what period of time and on what notice?

New York City.   G. H. W.

To the above the Adjutant General has furnished the following reply.

The Comptroller of the Treasury in a decision dated December 18, 1912, states that:

"The date from which an enlisted man is entitled to be paid is the date upon which he takes the oath of allegiance, except in those rare cases where it is affirmatively shown that the enlistment contract was completed and the man's status changed from that of a civilian to that of a soldier by some act other than the taking of the oath, such as actual entry upon duty with the knowledge and consent of the proper authorities, in which cases payment should be allowed from date of such act regardless of the date of application."

The case of the soldier referred to in paragraph one is not given a sufficient description to enable this office to express a definite opinion. If the soldier was in the enlisted reserve he would be entitled to pay from the date of reporting for active duty.

With respect to (2): In time of war or threatened hostilities the President may order members of the Officers' Reserve Corps to active duty with any of the military forces of the United States and in time of peace they may be called to active duty for a short period of training each year. The plans for annual training for reserve officers have not been completed and necessarily must await further legislation before final action. It is contemplated, however, that such training will be given next year and that all line officers and a great many of the staff

27th Division History

Endorsed by Major-General John F. O'Ryan

BEING the only **authentic History** of this **Famous Division**. From its send off to the stupendous welcome home parade, every period of its activities, here and abroad, is covered. Over **300** full and half page illustrations, including all **official photographs** of the Division in France. Full record of decorations and citations.

This book is one that no man who served or was connected with the 27th Division at any time should be without. Printed on heavily coated paper, bound in cloth.

This edition is limited and to insure prompt receipt of your copy fill out and mail enclosed coupon with money order at once.

```
-------------------- COUPON --------------------
ALEXANDER STARLIGHT, 981 Seneca Avenue, Brooklyn, N. Y.
  I enclose $3.50, for which send me copy of the
  PICTORIAL  HISTORY  OF  27th  DIVISION

Name_____

Address_____
```

corps officers will be included. If such training is decided upon, sufficient advance notice will be given in order to enable reserve officers to make proper arrangements. Every effort will be made to cause as little inconvenience as possible to those designated for such training.

Ladies' Auxiliaries

To the Editor: Can you furnish me information relative to starting a ladies' auxiliary to a Legion post?
Reading, Mass.   DOROTHY F. MORSE.

At a recent meeting of the National Executive Committee it was decided that the National Organization should encourage in every way the formation of women's auxiliaries of local posts; but this is a matter for the attention of local posts. We suggest that you get in touch with the state secretary of The American Legion in your state.

Tank Corps Camp

To the Editor: Has the tank corps a training camp now? If so, where is it located and what are the present training activities?
                              DONALD MCGRAW.
St. Louis, Mo.

Camp Mead, Md., is the present tank training center for the United States, and 600 men are now in training there.
(*Continued on page 32*)

AMERICA'S ARMY MUST FIGHT ON
ʟ(*Continued from page 9*)

society; second, legislation designed to benefit those who were disabled in the service; and third, legislation on the military policy of the country, dictated by the experiences of the recent war. The wishes of the Legion, as expressed by their representatives at Minneapolis, will get the immediate attention of your Legislative Committee.

I feel also that I should remark on the action of the convention in recognizing the Woman's Auxiliary of the American Legion, to which are eligible the wives, mothers, sisters and daughters of Legion members or men who lost their lives in service during the war. This organization has before it a great future, and can be made, and will be made, I know, a worthy helpmeet of the Legion in spreading the voice and will of a better Americanism.

A man is known by the enemies he makes, someone has said. The same is true of an organization. The Legion is known by its foes. The murder of Legionnaires in the state of Washington at the hands of Red radicals of the I. W. W. type, the news of which shocked the convention on Armistice Day, is a challenge the Legion accepts. We shall not belie the great principles for which we stand, by overstepping the bonds of law in dealing with this type of enemy, but the battle is on and the Legion shall not relent until America is purged, hide and hair, of every member of the I. W. W. and Bolshevik breed.

FIND YOUR BUDDY

MISSING: William Jack Maloney, discharged from service about September 1, 1919, and started from New York to Detroit to seek work as a machinist. His wife, Mrs. W. J. Maloney, 242 First Street, Newark, N. J., has not heard from him since.

William Jack Maloney

JEFFERSON DAVIS HENDERSON, 34 years old, served in French Foreign Legion two years prior to America's entry into war and was wounded three times. Incapacitated for line duty, was discharged from French service in 1917 and joined American Quartermaster Corps in France. Last heard from at Bennetable, Cote d'Or, in May, 1919. Address his mother, Mrs. Amelia J. Henderson, 3222 Calumet Avenue, Chicago.

M COMPANY, 101ST INFANTRY—Does anyone know the particulars of the death of Private Frederick A. Busby, successively reported missing in action, wounded, and killed? He was last seen in the Meuse-Argonne attack on the morning of October 24. Address, Earl O. Brown, 50 Southworth Street, Williamstown, Mass.

MISSING: Ordnance Sergeant W. A. Brindle, 305th Mobile Repair Shop, Eighteenth Division. Last heard from May 9, 1919, at Brest. Letters returned to parents marked "Returned to U. S. A. with Casual Company No. 3." Efforts to locate him through War Department or Red Cross channels have failed. Address, Mrs. B. D. Brindle, 1109 West Twenty-sixth Street, Erie, Pa.

MISSING: Harvey McClintock, Jr., 17 years old, left home in July, 1918, and wrote his parents from Dallas, Tex., that he had enlisted in the field artillery of the Regular Army, and was sailing for France in a month. His parents never heard from him again. Address, Harvey McClintock, Moran, Tex.

LINCOLN COHEN, formerly Fourth Infantry. The man you met on the road to La Charmel just before the fight there in July, 1918, has lost your address, and wants to hear from you. Address, L. J. Spartanzer, Bozeman, Mont.

EDWARD DUFFY, who served in France with the Signal Corps, and who was sick in Base Hospital 38 at Nantes, is asked to write John A. Usher, 7504 Limehilm Pike, Philadelphia.

HEADQUARTERS TROOP, 95TH DIVISION—Former Second Lieutenant W. E. Bradbury, Robinson, Ill., wants to hear from the men of his old command. He was in the hospital at Camp Sherman when the division was demobilized and consequently was unable to get the home addresses of his men before they were mustered out.

MISSING: Private Carmine De Peo, A Company, 106th Infantry. Went to France with that regiment in May, 1918, and last heard from on September 21, when the regiment was fighting on the British front. Address Rev. M. A. Price, 1340 Division Street, Portland, Ore.

COMPANY C, 304TH FIELD SIGNAL BATTALION.—Mrs. E. A. Krengel, 412 Eveshane Avenue, Govans, Md., wants to hear from men who can tell her how her son, Corporal Edgar R. Krengel, was killed. Corporal Krengel used to write home about a buddy whose last name was Edwards. Mrs. Krengel would like to hear from him.

JOSEPH POBACK, formerly of Company F, Ninth Infantry, your pal A. Bronson, who last heard from you when you had been wounded and were in a hospital, wants you to write. His address is 214 Shotwell Park, Syracuse, N. Y.

WILLIAM SPRINGETT, New York City, former sergeant E Company, 47th Infantry, and EDWARD KULMAN, Wheeling, W. Va., former sergeant, B Company, 39th Infantry, write your old pal, H. MacLeod, 9 Annapolis Street, Dorchester, Mass.

HEADQUARTERS COMPANY, 102d INFANTRY.—Will the men who were with Private Le Verne A. Belding when he was wounded communicate with his mother, Mrs. H. H. Belding, Waucoma, Ia.?

JOSEPH CALLAHAN, formerly E Company, 107th Infantry, believed to be in New York, write or telephone your buddy, E. D. O'Dell, care *Vogue*, 19 West 44th Street, New York City.

WALTER L. JONES, formerly Ambulance Company No. 39, last heard of at Is-sur-Tille, July 12, 1919, write your sister, Helen, 239 Baker Avenue, Syracuse, N. Y.

ALFRED T. TEW and his brother ARTHUR P. TEW, Medical Corps, may have their discharge certificates by writing H. W. Miller, 14105 Idarose Avenue, Cleveland, Ohio.

MAJOR JOHN C. FAIRFAX, U. S. A., served with Second Ammunition Train in France, write Joseph V. Ackerman, U. S. Army Recruiting Station, Uniontown, Pa.

JOHN A. HEINS, D. Company, 11th Marines, write Elmer R. Shambough, Norristown, Pa.

(Continued on page 33)

THE VOICE OF THE NEW DAY

(Continued from page 8)

The American Legion before the new National Executive Committee at its first meeting, which was held in Minneapolis the day after the convention adjourned.

Th committee viewed the matter in the same light and empowered the National Commander to nominate members proposed for the commission. This Mr. D'Olier intends to do as soon as he finds time to canvass the country in a search for the ablest and most active men he can lay hands on. He will weigh with care his selections. Several names, all of men known nationally, have been suggested. At the earliest practicable date the personnel of the commission will be announced, and the ground will be broken at once for the laying of the foundation for a structure which shall preach the doctrines and safeguard the legacies of Americanism in every nook and crevice of the nation.

In speaking in such detail of the resolution creating the National Americanism Commission of The American Legion, it has not been my design to exalt that act of the convention above the others. It is submitted only because of its comprehensive scope, and as a fair sample of the goods delivered. A perusal of any or all of the recommendations of the convening body should convince the most skeptical that the Legion seeks little for itself or its members other than that which shall accrue to all Americans from the making of a better and more wholesome America.

It passed over the bonus question, for example, expressing the sentiment that to put a cash value on the services freely tendered the country in time of war would dishonor that service. While recognizing the manifest injustice of a situation which sent the soldier to war to fight for a dollar a day, while the slacker and "industrially independent" remained amid the comforts at home, and as somebody remarked, "fought for higher wages," the Legion took the broad and patriotic view of the matter.

The recommendations regarding beneficial legislation dealt first with the disabled who have received such negligent attention at the hands of the government agencies charged with administering their affairs. The convention backed the recommendations of THE AMERICAN LEGION WEEKLY for more just and efficient conduct of the Federal Board for Vocational Education and the War Risk Insurance Bureau. The second consideration of the beneficial legislative program urged the passage by Congress of a bill to enable veterans to borrow money from the government to acquire land and build city and farm homes.

THE recommendations on military policy recognized the obligation of every man of military age to serve, and urged laws to enforce that obligation by dealing harshly with slackers and conscientious objectors. Military *training* for all was advocated, in order that the nation may not suffer "the bitter experience in the cost of unpreparedness" it suffered in the recent war. The Legion opposed compulsory military *service* in time of peace. It recognized the importance of the air service and asked that it be made a separate department from the Army and Navy, under the control of a new member of the Cabinet.

Such is the nature of the program to which the Legion pledges its one million members, a number which the National Commander hopes to see reach two million in the coming year. It embodies a gospel which the Rev. John W. Inzer, of Alabama, one of the leading figures of the convention, declared, "It shall afford me more satisfaction to preach than any other gospel on earth, save that of the Lord Jesus Christ."

It is, however, as yet only a gospel. It is the task of the Legion to make it a fact. One must not beguile himself into the belief that the great projects outlined by the convention will achieve themselves, for they will not. The work has been outlined and the instruments for its accomplishment placed in our hands. At the Minneapolis convention the Legion won the confidence of the nation. It must not fail that trust.

PRINCE OF WALES AND GOOD FELLOWS

(Continued from page 14)

extraordinarily pretty thing. And what does he do, the beggar?" The correspondent looked fondly at the object of his phillipic a few yards away. "Doesn't the good fellow send word that he wants to meet her. It amounts to a royal summons, you know. And that's the last I saw of her, will you believe me?"

And there also was that town in Alberta, and another pair of eyes. The royal motor was stopped, and the parade halted with it. A messenger ran to the sidewalk. The girl, with an overwhelming shyness, came to the side of the car ablush in her hour of surprising triumph.

"You are coming to the dance tonight?" His Highness asked.

She had not been invited.

"Then I invite you, and I hope you come," he urged. He danced seven times with her that night. And if that isn't a good girl spoiled for her insular sphere, then we err greatly. The blades of Alberta will be so many rummies to her. She has danced with her king.

In good time he will ascend the throne of Britain, with all its subject millions, and when he does he will know this side of the Atlantic not as a splotch of color on a map but as a reality translated in terms of city and plain and musical waters and God-believing people.

What is more, perhaps, is that to this side of the Atlantic he will be something more than a distant figure, sitting aloof from the affairs of men. He will know his soldiery not as a mass but as very human units, cold to sophistry and cant, but warm to him who speaks their language as does Albert Edward, who hates reveille and loves the ladies.

A dinner to the ex-service men of the Wanamaker Store was given by Thomas B. Wanamaker Post No. 413, New York. Major General Alexander and Major General O'Ryan spoke to the men.

THE GREAT "PAPER BULLET" DRIVE

(Continued from page 10)

ally was rewarded by a good laugh.

An Auzzie is a kind of a cousin, somehow.

THREE years after the first copy of the *Aerial Messenger* appeared I ran into an Auzzie at a little town called Villers-Bretenaux. He had one in his pack and he had it all translated into English.

Carefully and painstakingly had heearthed a Fritz and put him to work. The last sentence was:

"Are you a brave man or a coward? Your country is not England's country."

Now the Auzzie is almost a human being. This particular one regarded that as a sacred souvenir. It gave him something to laugh at. And laughs in the duckboards in front of Villers-Bretenaux were scarce. Fritz's *Aerial Messenger* contained some good lines, but it had the wrong audience. Its work was ineffective but amusing.

It took Jerry three years to learn to translate the same document into English. The translation in excellent Yankee vernacular that appears on page 10—it must be admitted—is familiar to most everyone who hit the Verdun front in the fall of 1918.

It also was familiar to some who were hit on the Verdun front about that time and to everyone who went over on that long winging front between St. Mihiel and Pont-a-Mousson. It was familiar to those who were left silent on that front between civilization and chaos.

The little white leaflets which came down from the sky from the low-flying Jerry planes! The editor of the *Aerial Messenger* hadn't been long getting the A. E. F. on the mailing list. He had profited by three years' experience with the British, and some of his stuff was not so bad, as humorous articles went those days.

Jerry had hived the lingo of the American soldier, hived it suspiciously well sometimes. That made you cuss and wonder how he'd done it. You were sore at the familiarity he showed in calling you "you fellows."

I REMEMBER once when some came down near Limey. It was plausibly written, one of Jerry's best efforts, in fact. A copy was taken to the captain. The old man put on his spectacles and read it through.

"Hold the company at mess tonight, sergeant," he said. "Fall them in ten minutes early."

"Men," said the captain that evening. Mine was the kind of a captain that didn't say, "boys." "Men, I'm going to give you a good laugh. You've got it coming. This thing here"—he indicated the leaflet—"was dropped all around the premises today. It's the kind of thing you've got to fight. The best way to fight it is to read it over carefully and realize there is something very, very funny about it. Now let's go over it together. Anybody who has a sheet get it out."

The captain went over it paragraph by paragraph and we laughed away any

of the poison that might have lurked there.

"Sergeant, ask the men if there are any questions?" said the old man as he wiped his glasses and put them in the old shagreen case.

Down at the end of the line Private (second class) O'Connell piped up in a high Hibernian voice:

"Captain, sir, can I keep mine as a souvenir?"

"Good idea, O'Connell. I believe I'll keep mine and send it home to the kids."

Second Lieutenant Roxby, who censored the company mail, must have found a lot of letters written on the back of Jerry's offering that week.

YOU see, it was a case of wrong audience. The play was all right, for actually Jerry's effort was good, but his chances went up in laughter.

Such was the simple secret of America's successful war against the deadly assault of "paper bullets." A barrage of paper bullets, probably no better charged than those that came over Limey that day, broke the Italian front in 1917, and had it not been for British and French divisions hastily transported to Italy that sunny land would have been another Belgium. The Italian soldiers constituted a "right" audience, from the German point of view. Orders had gone out placing severe penalties on reading the propaganda that came over. Human nature was being read upside down. A man never wants to do anything half so bad as when he is told he can't do it.

Italian troops read the leaflets secretly and they made a great impression, the very impression the Germans wanted them to make. What Italy needed then was a few men like our old captain, who would have laughed the German propagandists' claims away.

Our propaganda did the work it was written to do because the Germans adopted Italian tactics. Under penalty of death the Jerry soldier read our stuff, and for no other reason than because he was told he could not. Again, Jerry lacked a sense of humor.

There is a wooden cross near Thiaucourt, and on it is the aluminum identification disk of Private (second class) O'Connell. Before we buried him we took a souvenir from his pocket and sent it home. It asked if he was a brave man or a coward. Before he died he had read it and laughed, and battles have been won with such.

MISSING: William W. Adget, formerly 107th Trench Mortar Battalion, Thirty-second Division. On his return from France, Adget was discharged at Camp Grant, Ill., on Sept. 9, 1919. His family has had no word from him since. Address his mother, Mrs. Ben Adget, 832

Wm. W. Adget.

Clermont Street, Antigo, Wis.

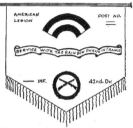

INFORMATION

(Continued from page 28)

Veterans' Education

To the Editor: Can you give me any information relative to the nine months educational course to be given to all veterans of the war?
Bellevue, Pa.   J. A. BLAST.

Senate Bill No. 3006, now before the Senate Committee on Military Affairs, proposes nine months educational and apprenticeship training at government expense for all veterans honorably discharged after at least sixty days actual service in the military or naval forces of the United States in the war with Germany. Veterans who apply for this training are to receive transportation to the college, school, business or apprenticeship institution which they select and $60 a month compensation for a period not to exceed nine months. A list of approved institutions for the attendance of veterans is to be prepared by a Federal Board for War Service Educational Facilities composed of the Secretary of War, the Secretary of the Navy, and four citizens, all ex-service men, appointed by the President with the advice and consent of the Senate.

Twelfth Division

To the Editor: What was the Twelfth Division? Did it serve overseas?
Baltimore, Md.   R. T. S.

The Twelfth Division was a Regular Army Division, formed at Camp Devens, Mass. It did not serve overseas.

Mileage

To the Editor: I was discharged from the Service February 1, at Garden City, L. I. At that time the government allowed 3½ cents a mile mileage. Soon thereafter mileage allowance was increased to 5 cents a mile. Can I collect the difference?
Brunswick, Mo.   G. STANBUS.

Yes. Affidavit, Form DS-ODF-2847, must be executed and sworn to before a notary public. Your original discharge certificate or a true copy of same, certified by a recruiting officer, should be forwarded with affidavit to the Zone Finance Office, Travel Allowance Section, Lemon Building, Washington, D. C.

American Legion Emblem

To the Editor: Has an American Legion navy button been issued?
Lockport, Ill.   E. A. CARY, JR.

No. The American Legion has but one emblem for all branches of the service. It is a button, three-quarters of an inch in diameter, consisting of a central small replica of the regulation bronze five-pointed star discharge button, surrounded by a narrow circular band of blue enamel containing the words "American Legion" in gold letters. The button has a fluted gold edge. The central replica of the discharge button is silver instead of bronze for members of the Legion who were wounded in the service. Pins, instead of buttons, of the same design are provided for women members.

Lost A. E. F. Mail

To the Editor: Kindly inform me to whom to write in order to recover mail sent me while in France, but never received.
Racine, Wis.   B. BENSINGER.

Write the Central Directory Service, care of Postmaster, Hoboken, N. J., describing lost letters or packages as fully as possible.

Sale of Army Automobiles

To the Editor: I understand the War Department is to place on sale new Dodge touring cars in khaki color with standardized parts. These machines were originally intended for use abroad for army officers and are now being offered for sale to ex-service men for either $400 or $600. Can you give me further information regarding same?
Norwich, Conn.   S. CRAMER.

The following information is supplied by the Quartermaster General, Director of Purchase and Storage, War Department, in reply to the above and to the questions of C. T. Melvin, Shortsville, N. Y., J. D. Henderson, Herkimer, N. Y., and W. M. Tappan, Holland, Mich.:

"It is not the policy of the War Department to dispose of its new Dodge equipment, inasmuch as the Dodge has been adopted as 'Standard Equipment' for the use of the Army. The Motor Transport Corps, Seventh and B Sts., N. W., Washington, D. C., may possibly be disposing of a limited quantity of unserviceable Dodge cars, at the sales which this corps is conducting throughout the United States, and it is suggested that if the members of The American Legion are interested in that class of vehicles they communicate their desires to the Motor Transport Corps."

S. A. T. C.

To the Editor: Will you kindly tell me whether members of the S. A. T. C. are entitled to the army button?
Middleburg, Va.   LEGION MEMBER.

No.

Uniform after Discharge

To the Editor: How long after discharge may a member of the United States Naval Reserve wear his uniform?
Providence, R. I.   J. J. BRADLEY.

Three months.

SERGEANT MAJOR CHARLES E. JUNE, Fourth Engineers, write Virginia S. Danser, John Sealy Hospital, Galveston, Tex.

80TH COMPANY, 6TH MARINES—Anyone who knew Corporal Harley H. Stone, who was killed in action in June or July, 1918, write his brother, Allen J. Stone, Effingham, Ill.

MORRIS RIECHELSON, formerly of Battery B, Fifteenth Field Artillery, and who came from France with Casual Company 1417. Anyone who knows of his whereabouts is asked to write F. Hatfield, 807 North Third Street, Springfield, Ill.

FIND YOUR BUDDY

(Continued from page 29)

MISSING: Lieut. Ivan Andrew Roberts, Twenty-seventh Aero Squadron, First Pursuit Group, missing in action north of Sevry, September 25, 1918. Flew over German lines on that date. Never seen afterwards. Message dropped by enemy flier stated that an "Aviator Roberts" died October 7. Anyone in possession of further information should write to National Headquarters, American Legion, 19 West Forty-fourth Street, New York City, who will notify family.

Lieut. Ivan Andrew Roberts

E COMPANY, 166TH INFANTRY.—Mrs. Lydia Hauser, Melbourne, Iowa, writes: "I have been extremely interested in your 'Find Your Buddy' column, as I, too, have lost through this war. I am so anxious to learn more concerning the wounding and death of my husband, Private Paul F. Hauser, Company E, 166th Infantry, 42nd Division. I was officially notified that he died of wounds, August 8, 1918, but I have been unable to learn anything as to how or where he fell. If there are any of his buddies who can tell me anything I will be truly grateful.

L COMPANY, 138TH INFANTRY.—W. S. Bates, athletic director of Southwestern College, Winfield, Kans., would like to hear from anyone who has particulars of the death of his brother, Corporal Perry J. Bates, who was killed in a raid in the Vosges on July 13, 1918.

K COMPANY, 7TH INFANTRY.—The sister of Sergeant Fred O. Kent, reported killed in action, October 12, 1918, would like to hear from anyone who can tell her any details of the engagement in which he met his death. Address, Hazel M. Kent, 5012 North Eleventh Street, Philadelphia.

I COMPANY, 311TH INFANTRY.—Information sought concerning death of Private John D. Weinman; wounded and taken to Base Hospital 48 where he recovered and was assigned to E-9 Unit. Later was taken with measles and is supposed to have died in Base Hospital 50. Parents were informed he was buried at Mesves, Nievre. Inquiry of the Graves Registration Bureau and the Red Cross has elicited no information. Address, Joseph P. Craugh, Secretary, Johnson-Costello Post, American Legion, Penn Yan, N. Y.

ED MELIA, or anyone who knows of his whereabouts, is asked to write Mrs. E. H. Melia, 1230 Long Street, Columbus, Ohio.

LETTERS FROM READERS

(*Continued from page 26*)

Hews to the Line

To the Editor: THE AMERICAN LEGION
WEEKLY hews to the line and is in every
way the proper paper for the expression
of the views of us former service men on
conditions during and after the war.
Erie, Kans.   THOMAS A. STRATTON.

Congratulations

To the Editor: I take the liberty of
congratulating THE AMERICAN LEGION
WEEKLY on the splendid article, "A
Starting Point for Slacker Drives."
Highland Park, Mich.   WILLIAM F. ALLEN.

"Second the Motion"

To the Editor: I just received my October 31 copy and have read only the
first article, "What's Wrong with War
Risk?" I cannot settle myself to read
the other articles until I get this hearty
"Second the Motion" out of my system.
That one article is worth the entire
year's dues we are collecting from our
Zanesville members. I converted my
insurance in May and dues still are coming for the monthly payments. I cannot
get answers to any of my letters, and I
am constantly wondering where I stand.
Zanesville, Ohio.   PERRY D. GATH.

Every Page Interesting

To the Editor: I have been reading
THE AMERICAN LEGION WEEKLY for
some time, and I want to tell you how
much I enjoy it. Every page is interesting and I look forward to it each week.
Randolph, Vermont.   ROY M. BRAGG.

With the Haircut

To the Editor: In my barber shop I
have two daily newspapers and four
magazines, but THE AMERICAN LEGION
WEEKLY is the most sought for of them
all. They all like to read it.
Eldridge, Iowa.   L. N. MASTERSON.

From the Old Dominion State

To the Editor: Just a line to tell you
that your WEEKLY (I mean "ours") is
read and appreciated by a lot of us in
the "Old Dominion State." It improves
with each number. Keep up the poetry
page, also the Find Your Buddy column.
East Radford, Va.   H. R. FRENCH.

A Tribute

To the Editor: I have taken several
magazines in my life and I am a great
reader, but there is not one that I read
with more interest than THE AMERICAN
LEGION WEEKLY. Every American
should have the valuable paper in his
home. Long live The American Legion.
Bolivar, Mo.   HENRY C. KUHN.

"May It Live Forever"

To the Editor: I may say for the 6,000
Lehigh County, Pennsylvania, soldiers
that THE AMERICAN LEGION WEEKLY is
the best paper we have ever read or ever
expect to read. May it live forever.
Allentown, Pa.   EARLE L. WEAVER.

Can't Afford to Miss It

To the Editor: I am enclosing money for
my subscription. Have delayed subscribing
because of uncertainty as to where I shall
finally settle, but I shall make room for
the winter and don't feel that I can afford
to miss the WEEKLY, for it has already
proven invaluable to me.

The greatest task of the Legion and
its "voice" will be to combat the unneces-
sary, non-constructive and exceedingly
injurious un-American and unpatriotic
"calamity howling," which is too frequently heard from the ex-service man as
well as others.

One hears bolshevist remarks from men
who would be quite indignant if you were
to suggest they lacked patriotism. There
are many unfortunate conditions arising
out of the tremendous task for which our
peace-loving country was certainly not
prepared, and one is likely to forget the
fact that the efficient work of the government far overbalanced its inefficiency.
It is unfortunate that the less efficient
circumstances are those which have
most serious bearing on individual cases,
and some cases are very provoking and
frequently most sympathetic. But we
have a great big organization now which
can work wonders toward clearing up
such conditions, The American Legion,
and it is up to us to show our faith in our
Legion and in our government by stop-
ping this calamity howling, which gains us
nothing, and going about the betterment
of conditions in a more practical manner,
through the Legion, through THE AMERI-
CAN LEGION WEEKLY, through our
Congressmen.
              CARLETON D. LATHROP.
Scottsbluff, Neb.

Saw an Old "Home"

To the Editor: I was very much surprised when I picked up my copy of THE
AMERICAN LEGION WEEKLY of October
17 to see one of my old homes staring me in
the face. The dugouts and shelters near
Flirey, France, or to be exact, on the road
from Flirey to Bernecourt, pictured on
page 21, were occupied by Company B,
Fifth Engineers, Seventh Division, of
which I was a member, from December
2 to December 7, 1918. We were policing
up duds and hand grenades and other
explosives left in Flirey and making it
generally safe for the "Democrats."
I have a picture of this place which proves
that our friend W. J. Aylward is some
artist. It is readily recognized.
              WILLIAM M. WHITAKER.
Russellville, Ky.

Up to the Minute

To the Editor: I get much pleasure
and enjoyment out of THE AMERICAN
LEGION WEEKLY, as do others of my
post. It is an up-to-the-minute, snappy
magazine, in which I take more pride
than all the rest of the magazines I get.
It is tempered with just enough adventur-
ous and exciting fiction to satisfy the
cravings of ex-service men along that
line and to balance the more serious
topics of universal discussion.
Marblehead, Mass.   P. O. POTTER.

Herman's Famous

STYLE

"291"

Civilian Model
Made of Gun Metal Leather. Heavy Single Sole

"In War and in Peace"—

HERMAN'S SHOES

CIVILIAN STYLES—ARMY STYLES

TODAY millions of American men—men who have come home from the War and men who couldn't go to the War—are wearing Herman's Shoes.

The ex-soldiers are finding it a joy to slip their feet into Herman's *Civilian* models having the same comfort and wonderful wearing qualities as the Herman's U. S. Army Shoes they wore in the Service, with the added attraction of shapely foreparts and up-to-the-minute style features throughout.

The average man *everywhere* finds Herman's Civilian Styles unexcelled for business and dress—and he also discovers in the famous Herman's U. S. Army Shoes the finest footwear for heavy work and outdoor pleasures he can possibly obtain.

Herman's Shoes are sold in 8000 retail stores. If you are not near one, we will fit you correctly and quickly through our MAIL ORDER DEP'T at Boston. SEND FOR CATALOG.

JOSEPH M. HERMAN SHOE CO.

1026 ALBANY BLDG., BOSTON, MASS.

CPSIA information can be obtained
at www.ICGtesting.com
Printed in the USA
BVHW071358231118
533754BV00030B/3526/P